Get More Like Jesus
While Watching TV

Get More Like Jesus While Watching TV

Nick Pollard and
Steve Couch

Authentic

www.DamarisBooks.com

First published in 2005 by Damaris Books, an imprint of Authentic
Media, 9 Holdom Avenue, Bletchley, Milton Keynes, Bucks, MK1
1QR, UK and PO Box 1047, Waynesboro,
GA 30830-2047, USA.

British Library Cataloguing in Publication Data
A catalogue record for this book is available
from the British Library.

1-904753-08-6

Cover design by fourninezero design.
Print management by Adare Carwin
Printed in the UK by Haynes, Sparkford, Yeovil, Somerset

For Carol, who patiently answers the constant
question 'Who is that actor?'
and
For Ann, whose company improves any TV show

Contents

Acknowledgements

My father-in-law gets very frustrated by a trend in current TV broadcasting. At the end of every programme, broadcasters are legally obliged to show the credits, saying who did what to make the show possible. But increasingly – and particularly on shows aimed at children and teenagers – as the credits roll, the image is reduced to a fraction of the available size. At the same time, most of the screen is filled with a perma-grinning presenter who tells us about the exciting and innovative shows that are coming next. The TV channels are obviously worried about losing viewers during the 'dull bits', and work hard to keep a fast-moving, go-getting feel to their between-show links. The problem is, there are some people (my father-in-law among them) who are genuinely interested in reading the credits. If I'm honest, I share this tendency. Sometimes I enjoy just looking out for unusual or unfortunate names – and I was very excited as a teenager to spot that the video editor of *Alas Smith and Jones* was called Steve Couch. I have followed my namesake's career in end-credits ever since. There is also somebody important who works for *Sky News* called Nick Pollard – but he is nothing to do with the Nick Pollard who has co-written this book.

But there is a more important function to these credits,

which is possibly why my father-in-law gets so irate at their relegation to the corner of the screen. It is important to give recognition when someone has worked hard to make something happen. There are several people who deserve to be mentioned for the part they played in bringing this book to fruition. Some readers will possibly want to skip this part, just as they would rather listen to the presenters than watch the end credits, but if you are interested in credit being given where it is due, then this is what you should know.

Originally this book was going to be written by a number of people, after Nick and I had shaped the structure. However, when we started to receive their completed chapters, we realised that the argument of the book just wasn't holding together the way it was meant to. It was no fault of the writers or their material, but we realised that we needed to rewrite the book with fewer hands. We are very grateful to Di Archer, Elaine Duncan, Nigel Pollock and Anna Robbins for their hard work which never made it to the printed page. We are particularly indebted to Di Archer and her husband Graham as well for their encouragement of this project from a very early stage. Their belief in the concept of this book played an important part in making it actually happen.

Caroline Puntis, Ian Hamlin and Louise Crook very kindly agreed to us reprinting their study guides from www.culturewatch.org, which we are very grateful for. Thanks should also go to our Damaris colleague Tony Watkins, who does a fantastic job editing the Culturewatch site, which plays a major part in helping us and others to think about popular culture with God's eyes on. He has also made some very helpful observations on the text at various stages, particularly concerning the material on the book of Daniel in chapter 3. We would also like to thank Julian Weisserhorn for his perceptive observations on several chapters, which have helped us to clarify our argument.

Of our other Damaris colleagues, Louise Crook (again) made some excellent contributions to the study questions at the end of the chapters, Peter S. Williams has been a helpful sounding board throughout, suffering my numerous interruptions with cheerful good grace, and Steve Alexander read through the almost-final version of the text, looking for glitches. Throughout the whole lengthy gestation period of this book, Kate Laver has been invaluable in taking care of all of the administrative issues that surround getting a book published, and is owed a great debt of thanks. We should also thank our new partners at Authentic Media, particularly Malcolm Down and Liz Williams, for their expert advice in the world of publishing.

Originally this book was going to be published by Damaris and distributed by IVP, until financial realities forced a change of strategy. We would like to thank everyone at IVP, particularly Brian Wilson and Tim Banting, for their gracious response to our decision to license our book publishing to Authentic. They gave us a lot of encouragement and advice concerning this title, and had worked hard selling the book into bookshops, only to lose the book to another company. Their willingness to see our side of the situation and their desire for whatever best helped God's kingdom, over and above their profit margins, were exemplary. We were very grateful to them for making a difficult situation a little easier. Similarly, John Laister and the team at AD Publishing Services had also been a joy to work with. The fact that we no longer work with either ADPS or IVP is Damaris' only downside of our move to Authentic.

Nick wants to thank his children, Luke and Lizzie, as

well as Lizzie's friend Steph Gordon, for their assistance in helping him find good TV-related examples. I'd like to thank my wife Ann for playing the same role in my research, although my son Peter's suggestions would probably have been more helpful if he had learned to talk yet.

While all of the above have played valuable roles in pruning and improving this book, it goes without saying that Nick and I are responsible for any errors or shortcomings that remain.

Finally, we should thank all the talented writers, directors, actors and TV executives who make excellent TV shows that help us to get more like Jesus – whether that was their intention or not!

Steve Couch, January 2005

Therefore, I urge you brothers [and sisters], in view of God's mercy, to offer your bodies as living sacrifices, holy and pleasing to God – which is your spiritual worship. Do not conform any longer to the pattern of this world, but be transformed by the renewing of your mind. Then you will be able to test what God's will is – his good, pleasing and perfect will.

Romans 12:1–2

Foreword
Four Ways to Watch
By Nick Pollard

Will you imagine a scene with me? It is the living room in a flat shared by four Christians. They are sitting down together in front of the TV. They are going to watch exactly the same programme, on exactly the same set, in exactly the same room. And yet it is going to have four very different effects upon them. Two of them are going to take significant steps forward in their walk with God – they are going to get more like Jesus. But two of them are going to go the other way. One of them will be aware of the presence of God as they watch the programme. One, by the end of the show, will feel that God is even more distant than ever. One will find that the TV sharpens their brain and enlivens it to think more deeply about living for Christ in today's world. And one will switch their brain even more fully into the off position as they become even more dull and lifeless.

What makes the difference between the four Christians? It is what is going on inside their heads as they watch the TV. It is their motivation for watching the programme. It is the way in which they watch it. So let's imagine that we can look inside each of the four people's heads and see what is going on.

The first Christian is watching TV because she appreciates the creativity and artistry that is expressed on the screen. She has understood the fact that all good art is an expression of the creativity that God put within us humans when he made us in his image. She knows that Christians are better placed than most to understand creativity, because of our intimate relationship with the Creator. And she knows that Christians should be the most appreciative of art because we know the Artist.

But she also knows that we live in a corrupted world in which men and women have chosen to go their own way, and to live without God – including in their creativity and artistry. She knows that there is a devil who seeks, as Jesus put it, to 'steal and kill and destroy' (John 10:10). He cannot create anything himself; he can only steal what God has created and corrupt it. And as he does, so he seeks to kill people's spiritual life and vitality, he destroys the good things that God has given us to enjoy. She knows that, while good art expresses something of God the creator, bad art expresses something of the devil the destroyer.

As she watches the TV she seeks to draw closer to God by discerning the good art and rejecting the bad. She rejoices in the creativity that God has given us all and she thanks God for all of his good gifts. She experiences something more of the presence of God. But she also prays that God will preserve her from the corruption of her creativity and artistry. And she prays for those whose art steals and kills and destroys.

The second Christian is watching TV because he wants to be more effective at reaching his friends with the gospel. He loves his friends and he wants them to experience God's love in their lives. But he knows that most of them are not really interested in hearing about Jesus – because their beliefs and values have been shaped in another way. And for most of them TV has played a significant part in that shaping process.

If he asks his friends what they believe about life, love, meaning, purpose, truth – in fact any of the big issues of life – he can see that their responses express ideas that have been reinforced, if not originated, by the programmes they watch. He is aware that these ideas are not usually expressed explicitly on the surface of the TV programmes. They are usually hidden in the underlying subtext of the show – in what is presented as normal and in what philosophers would call the 'assumed status' of the ideas.

So, as he watches the TV, he is actively trying to identify the underlying subtext of the programme. Looking beneath the surface he seeks to find the assumptions that the show is reinforcing. He is endeavouring to work out the effect of such a show on the beliefs and values of his friends. And he is considering ways in which he might use examples from the show to help them to think again about the assumptions that they have absorbed – and ultimately to think about the life and teaching of Jesus. He realises that this is not easy, so as he watches the TV he is also praying that God will sharpen his brain and enable him to think more deeply.

For him, like the first Christian, watching the TV is helping him to grow more like Jesus.

The third Christian doesn't really want to think at all. As far as he is concerned Frank Lloyd Wright[1] was correct when he described TV as 'chewing gum for the eyes'. And that's what he wants to do – to sit down for some mindless chewing in front of a screen. He wants something that will entertain him, something that will enable him to switch off his brain and relax. He doesn't intend to think or pray or do anything at all.

He watches TV because he wants to be amused. And

even that word describes what he is doing. Although we don't quite know the derivation of the word some say that it comes from two Greek words 'a' and 'mousa' meaning literally 'without thinking'; whereas others say that it comes from the ancient French 'a' and "muser" meaning literally 'to stupefy'. Either way, the word indicates the switching off of one's brain.

But, whatever his brain is doing while he is watching TV, someone else's brain has been working very hard. In fact lots of brains have been engaged in creating the programme that he is watching. The writers, producers, directors have all thought very carefully about the ideas, beliefs and values that this programme is expressing. And while this Christian has turned his brain off, to be amused, he is also opening himself wide to absorbing those ideas, beliefs and values. He is not discerning the good from the bad, the godly from the ungodly, the biblical from the unbiblical. He is simply letting the TV shape his mind, his heart, his soul.

The fourth Christian is thinking but may not really want other Christians to know what she is thinking. She is watching TV because she wants to fantasise about the story it tells. She wants to imagine that she is that girl who is with that boy who is madly in love with her. She wants to imagine that she is living the life that she sees portrayed.

She knows that this is not real. She knows that it is not actually helpful to her in her walk with God in the real world. She knows that her fantasies about the stories she watches are equivalent to the fantasies of her male friends that are more graphically based upon the pictures and images. She knows that what she is doing is the exact opposite of the prayer that Jesus gave. Jesus said 'lead me not into temptation', whereas she is seeking to lead herself into temptation. She wants to push the boundaries, to move closer, to try more.

For her, like the third Christian, watching the TV is helping her to grow less like Jesus.

I wonder, which of these four Christians is most like you? Probably, if you are like most of us, then you are a mixture of all four. Sometimes you watch TV like one of these people, sometimes like another, and at other times like several mixed together.

If that is so, then I think you will find this book particularly helpful. Steve and I, the authors of this book, are a bit like each of the four Christians I have described. We wrestle and struggle with following Christ in this TV-dominated world, and we are committed to thinking through what the Bible has to say about these issues. We are not going to give you simple answers – this is not a simple '10 easy steps' type of book. But this book will help you to think carefully and biblically about the way in which you watch TV. And it will help you to find out more about how you can get more like Jesus while watching TV.

Notes

1 Many people have used this phrase, and there are some who also claim authorship of it. The earliest use we are aware of was by the famous architect Frank Lloyd Wright.

1

Previously On . . .
In View of God's Mercy

Therefore, I urge you brothers [and sisters], in view of
God's mercy, to offer your bodies as living sacrifices, holy
and pleasing to God – which is your spiritual worship.
Do not conform any longer to the pattern of this world,
but be transformed by the renewing of your mind. Then
you will be able to test what God's will is – his good,
pleasing and perfect will.

Romans 12:1–2

Increasingly, TV companies are tending to make serials
rather than series. In a series, each episode stands alone.
Although there may be a common group of central
characters, there is no continuous narrative. Anybody
could tune in to any episode and understand what was
going on. Classic sitcoms such as *The Good Life* or *Dad's
Army*, or more recent shows such as *Men Behaving Badly*
or *Coupling* are examples of the series. Serials, on the
other hand, are more dependent on what has gone
before. This isn't to say that the problem faced by the
characters at the start of the episode won't be resolved by
the end, or that any single episode won't have a
satisfying pay-off, but nevertheless the big story is told

1

over many episodes. This means that if you want to understand what's going on, you need to know what has happened before. Shows like *The West Wing* and *24* commonly start each episode with a recap: a familiar cast-member's voice intones 'Previously on *The West Wing*' and we are shown a brief montage of scenes and incidents from recent episodes.

The Bible is more like a TV serial than a TV series. Although you can take individual parts of the Bible and understand them without reference to anything else, to get the most out of any passage, you need to be able to put it in context. In the rest of this book we explore the way we watch television. We are going to be thinking about what it means to bring the whole of our lives under God's control, including our TV habits. In particular we are going to be looking closely at one small snippet from the letter to the Romans – the first two verses of chapter 12. These two verses are going to be our guide to considering how watching TV can help us to become more like Jesus and more effective in sharing Jesus with other people. We're not claiming that reading this book will do all the hard work for you, but we do believe that the way we watch TV can help or hinder our growth as Christians.

The beginning of Romans 12 is a turning point in the letter, where Paul stops outlining the basic principles of the Gospel and starts to apply those principles, suggesting implications as he goes. Verse 1 begins 'Therefore, I urge you . . .' If we start our study with Romans 12:1–2, we can still get some benefit from the verses, but like a new viewer joining a TV show in the middle of a series, we can't expect to fully understand it unless we know what the 'Therefore' refers to. In the context of this book, think of this chapter as the familiar cast-member's voice summarising the argument of the preceding eleven chapters. OK, start up the theme tune, roll the titles, and cue the voiceover: 'Previously in Romans . . .'

Romans: the story so far

Paul wrote the letter to the Romans somewhere around AD 55, towards the end of his life. The letter contains the fullest, most detailed explanation of the gospel that the Bible gives us. Paul was writing to the Church in Rome, which he had always wanted to visit but had so far been unable to.[1] Paul is writing partly to address the needs of the Roman church, and partly setting out his credentials so that his ministry as an apostle will be more readily accepted once he finally gets there.

In simple terms, the main message of Romans can be divided into five sections, plus Paul's more personal greetings at the beginning and end of the letter:

- Our problem (1:18–3:20)
- God's solution (3:21–4:25)
- Our new status (5:1–8:39)
- Old ways and the new way (9:1–11:36)
- Changing channels: living God's way (12:1–15:13)

Let's take a look at what the Bible has to say in the sections leading up to our main verses.

Our problem (Romans 1:18–3:20)

Paul explains that we have a big problem – God is angry, and all of humanity is in the firing line. The problem is that we have failed to live up to God's standards. More than that, we have rebelled against him. 1:23 talks about people exchanging the glory of the immortal God for images made to look like mortal man and birds and animals and reptiles. We may never have crafted a golden statue of a calf to worship instead of God, but there are plenty of other things that we choose (consciously or without realising it) to build our lives around. It's easy for us to think that we aren't affected by the things we watch, but if that's the case why do manufacturers pay thousands of pounds every month for TV advertising? And why, now that technology exists to record TV shows while skipping over the adverts, are more and more manufacturers paying for product placement in top shows rather than sticking to traditional advertising? We are fooling ourselves if we try to claim that TV has no impact and influence in our lives.

Whatever it is that drives your life, whatever is most important to you, that is what you have exchanged God's glory for. We may live for pleasure, for money, even for our favourite TV shows, but if the thing that really drives us isn't God, then these verses apply to us. Verse 25 puts it more starkly: 'They have exchanged the truth of God for a lie, and worshipped and served created things rather than the Creator.' Paul is describing the basic human condition of rebellion against God – and it isn't pretty. No matter how hard we try, we can never manage to keep God's laws and live up to his standard. And the result of that is that we face God's anger and are under his judgement.

God's solution (Romans 3:21–4:25)

God knows that there is no way for us to be good enough under our own efforts, so he provides another way – someone who is good enough to be able to take our punishment for us. 3:23–24 sums up both the problem and the solution: 'for all have sinned and fall short of the glory of God, and are justified freely by his grace through the redemption that came by Christ Jesus.'

Time and again on TV dramas, we see people facing a hopeless situation and completely dependent on a heroic rescuer. Whether it is Jack Bauer in *24* thwarting terrorist plots, or the Tracey Brothers in *Thunderbirds* flying in to avert another crisis, the idea of the dramatic rescue of the helpless and hopeless is part of our cultural wallpaper.

This is nothing new – Romans chapter 4 explains that way back in early Old Testament times, Abraham was saved by faith in God rather than through his own deeds. God's plan has always been based on the same unchanging premise – humans are incapable of being good enough to earn our own salvation, so we need God (and in particular, Jesus) to come and do it for us. The point of the law was not to provide us with a way out of trouble, but to show us how far short of God's standards we fell (Romans 3:20). The angry God of judgement is also a patient God of mercy, who holds his judgement back, giving us the chance to change our ways.

Our new status (Romans 5:1–8:39)

Soap operas wouldn't work if people didn't keep on doing bad things. Every soap worth its salt has at least one character who is forever saying sorry for the things they have done and then going out and doing something just as bad. It seems that this type of person was prevalent at the time Romans was written. Some people misinterpreted Paul's argument to mean that anyone could do whatever they wanted. If our sins are going to be forgiven anyway, why not have a whale of a time and just give God more to forgive? Surely this would be a good thing, as it would make God's mercy even more impressive? Paul deals specifically with this argument in chapter 6, spelling out that God's grace does not give us a license to sin (Romans 6:1–2 and 6:15). When we were slaves to sin and impurity, the result was we became worse and worse (Romans 6:19); now that we have been released from sin's slavery, we are to offer ourselves as slaves to God, and to live lives that lead to holiness (Romans 6:22–23). We are still slaves, still bound to obey a master. The difference is that now it is God, rather than our selfish and sinful human nature, that calls the tune.[2]

Although God has already declared us righteous because of Jesus' death in our place, and although we will be made perfect once we get to heaven, that doesn't mean that we have nothing to get on with now. Notice in 6:22 that the benefit of our new life *leads to* holiness – it doesn't happen overnight. In Romans 5:1–5 Paul talks about the way that suffering for Jesus' sake develops our character, and this shows that Christian character is a work in progress.

Every week on *Changing Rooms*, two rooms in neighbouring houses are transformed by the vision of the show's designers. Sometimes the owners of the houses are delighted by the new look, and sometimes they are less than pleased. Occasionally (if the producers are really lucky) they cry. But the point is that the rooms aren't just there to look good on the telly. After the cameras have gone, people have to live in them (a fact which some of the designers seem to forget!) The Christian life isn't a quick fix over the course of a couple of days, and it isn't meant to just look good on the outside. It's not enough for us to do the equivalent of slapping on some paint and a few sheets of MDF to hide all the old rubbish underneath. To really transform a house takes time and effort, and it's the same when we get serious with God about changing our lives. But, like *Changing Rooms*, we aren't left to do it all ourselves. In the same way that the show's designers come up with a plan and join in the work, so God shows us what we need to do and helps us to get on with the job of sorting things out. God's plan is for us to live lives that bring him honour and which prepare us for the eternity we will spend with him. As Romans 8:18 spells out, the end result is going to be worth all the hard work we have to put in.

Old ways and the new way (Romans 9:1–11:36)

The church at Rome was made up of Jewish Christians and Gentile (i.e. non-Jewish) converts. Paul's letter reflects the cultural dispute that raged between those two groups in the early church. Paul has already touched on this division in Romans 3 and 4, but now in the three chapters immediately preceding our key verses, he returns to the problem. Many of the Jewish Christians felt that the Gentiles should submit themselves to all the old Jewish food laws and other regulations. Others (including Paul) argued that since Christ's death had done what the law could not and made salvation possible, it would be ridiculous to place the burden of keeping all the Jewish regulations on new Gentile converts. You can read more about how the early church leaders dealt with the Jew versus Gentile dilemma in Acts 15.

The situation in Rome, and elsewhere in the early church, is similar to the situation facing the two main human characters in the Sci-fi sitcom *Red Dwarf*.

In *Red Dwarf*, Dave Lister is the last human left alive. He was a lowly crew member on a deep space mining vessel (the 'Red Dwarf' of the title) belonging to the Jupiter Mining Corporation. Lister was forever being punished for breaking rules and disobeying orders, and was eventually put in suspended animation in a stasis field as a punishment for smuggling a cat onto the ship. But the punishment saved Lister's life, keeping him safe when the rest of the crew was killed by a radiation leak. Once the radiation had subsided to a safe level, Holly (the ship's computer) brought Lister out of stasis. Unfortunately this was three million years later. Not only were all of his friends dead, but the entire human race (apart from Lister) was extinct. Holly was able to create a holographic version of one – and only one – of the ship's crew to keep Lister company. However, he chose Arnold Rimmer, Lister's old roommate. Rimmer and Lister are polar opposites – Lister the archetypal slobbish and anarchic space-bum, and Rimmer an uptight control freak with an obsession for sticking to the regulations.

The regulations in *Red Dwarf* had become meaningless – there was no Jupiter Mining Corporation to report to, no authority to answer to, and yet Rimmer clung to the old rules, trying unsuccessfully to make Lister toe the line as well. Some of the Jewish Christians were trying to do much the same thing. It wasn't that there was no authority to report to any more – God was still very much in the picture – but the Church was facing the realisation that the old way of trying to earn God's favour by doing all the right things (and none of the wrong ones) had never worked, and wasn't the way to be saved. In fact, God's plan had always been to save us by his grace, rather than on the basis of our own merit. But his people were a little slow in realizing that!

In chapters 9 to 11, Paul considers how we understand God's mercy: why does God allow some of his chosen people to reject his mercy, while welcoming in some of those who, to Jewish minds at the time, were outside of his plan? 11:13–14 suggests that Paul believes his ministry to the Gentiles will ultimately lead other Jews back into God's mercy. 10:11–15 spells out our part in all this, whether we are Jewish Christians or Gentile Christians. We can only be saved if we put our faith in Jesus and call on his name. How can others be saved if nobody tells them about Jesus? Part of the dynamic, changed and changing Christian life that we are urged to embrace is to tell other people what Jesus has done for us and for them, and to offer them the chance to put their faith in him too.

Changing channels: living God's way

And that's where this book comes in. In view of God's mercy, we should want to become more effective for him. We should want God to use us to reach other people with the fantastic news that they can be rescued from sin and judgement. That involves us changing, and this book is about the changes – in our thinking and in actions – that we need to make.

Don't think these changes are to make ourselves feel that we can ever deserve Jesus' sacrifice – the whole point of the gospel is that we don't deserve it, and never can. Everything that follows is because of God's mercy, rather than our merit. The best we can manage is to be grateful and to try to please God in return. We pay him back for his great gift out of our poverty. This isn't 'paying him back' in the sense of paying the price for the goods we have received, like buying a flashy new widescreen TV from the local electrical superstore and paying off the cost over several months. Rather, this paying back is more like a small child who makes breakfast for his mum on Mothers' Day. The child's actions don't even begin to redress the balance for all the things that his mum does for him (and the breakfast may not even taste as nice as if she had done it herself), but he makes breakfast for his mum because he wants to show how much he loves her and appreciates all that she does for him. And this response, as inadequate as it is, delights his mum to her very soul.

The rest of this book helps us to think about how we can give God a Mothers' Day gift that he will love. It helps us to think how we should respond to the extraordinary mercy and love that God has lavished on us, and how we can become more effective for the sake of his kingdom. Being effective for God's kingdom doesn't mean having no time at all for the so-called trivial trappings of modern life, such as watching television. What it does mean is that all of those trivialities matter to God. There is no part of our lives that is too small for him to want to be involved, no part that he doesn't want us to do his way and for his glory. And that means putting him in charge of the TV remote control as well as the big decisions in life. What does that mean in practice? That's what this book is all about.

Study questions:

Why is God interested in our TV viewing? What do you think is his view of your TV habits?

What does it mean to put God in charge of the TV remote control?

What TV-related illustrations (other than the ones in this chapter) might you use to explain the gospel to your friends?

What are you hoping to get out of reading this book?

Notes

1 Romans 1:8,13,15 and 15:23
2 It should be noted that our slavery to God, paradoxically, brings a sense of freedom and liberation, as it releases us into the life that we were made to enjoy. Jesus said that he came to bring people 'life in all its fullness' (John 10:10), and Paul tells us that the Christian life is marked by joy (Galatians 5:22). Nevertheless, we find this only in a committed and obedient relationship with God, which Paul describes in Romans using the imagery of slavery.

2

A Very Peculiar Praxis
What Does it Mean to Offer Your Bodies as Living Sacrifices?

Therefore, I urge you brothers [and sisters], in view of God's mercy, to offer your bodies as living sacrifices, holy and pleasing to God – which is your spiritual worship. Do not conform any longer to the pattern of this world, but be transformed by the renewing of your mind. Then you will be able to test what God's will is – his good, pleasing and perfect will.

Romans 12:1–2

Each Christmas, the TV channels compete against one another to attract the most viewers, and films are a major weapon in that ratings war. The key to success for each television channel is not just securing the latest blockbuster release, but also judging the trends in TV watching in order to pick the best older films to re-run.

One film which is shown on TV almost every Christmas is Frank Capra's *It's a Wonderful Life*. This is perhaps the ultimate feel-good movie (despite some very dark moments) and was voted into 34th place in *Empire* magazine's 2004 readers' survey of the best films of all time.[1] However, it was not so highly rated when it was first released in 1946, and it owes much of its success to repeated broadcasts on TV during the 1970s (helped by a clerical error that allowed the copyright to lapse, allowing any TV station to show it without paying a fee). Thus it has become a TV classic, and practically everyone has seen it on the small screen at least once during one Christmas season or another.

One of the central themes in this film concerns what we do with our lives – indeed what we do with our bodies. At the beginning we meet Clarence, a disembodied angel.[2] Clarence is given a body in order to come to earth to save George (played by James Stewart). George has a body but wants to kill it, because he thinks he has wasted his life in his middle-American small-town, and feels that it would have been better if he had never been born.

This film is popular because it engages the viewers' emotions so powerfully – particularly in its heart-warming (and tear-jerking) final scene. But it is also significant for the way in which it demonstrates that the use of our bodies affects us and other people around us.

Choosing sides

The question of what we should do with our bodies and lives has been explored in many other TV shows. Characters in the cosmetic surgery drama *Nip/Tuck* suggest that we have a responsibility to our partner to look as good as possible, by any means possible. By contrast, in one episode of the comedy series *Scrubs* central character JD has to decide whether he is going to use his position as a doctor at a busy American hospital to boost profits or to help patients, regardless of whether or not they can afford their treatment. JD's struggle with the responsibility of his position finds an echo in the Bible, which tells us that we have been given bodies to enable us to live in God's world, and that we are responsible for how we use them. This is particularly evident in this phrase in Romans: 'offer your bodies as living sacrifices'.

In the last chapter we took an overview of Romans. The central section (Romans 5:1–8:39) tells us of the new life we receive when we become Christians. In the middle of that section is a crucial sentence, 'Do not offer the parts of your body to sin, as instruments of wickedness, but rather offer yourselves to God, as those who have been brought from death to life; and offer the parts of your body to him as instruments of righteousness' (Romans 6:13). So, we have a choice – we can offer our bodies to sin, which the Bible warns us against; or offer them to God, which the Bible encourages us to do. We don't have a choice about whether or not to offer our bodies at all, we can't avoid that. The only question is which way we will offer them.

The Greek word which is translated as 'offer' literally means 'place beside or near'. It is a word used to refer to bystanders who just happen to be nearby something as well as those who have specifically chosen to be there. As we live in this world we inevitably move about, so we can't help 'offering' our bodies. This might be like a bystander (we just happen to be somewhere without really thinking about it) or may be the result of a specific choice.

The Bible clearly tells us to be careful about how and where we offer our bodies. So, as we sit down to watch TV, we need to think about the programmes we are going to select. We need to choose programmes that are consistent with offering our bodies as instruments of righteousness, rather than with offering our bodies to sin.

For that reason we would advise against the popular practice of mindlessly flicking through the channels until you find something you might want to watch. Because sin is so attractive you will probably find that the programme which grabs your attention is likely to be one which is not good for you. Rather, we would suggest making a conscious decision about what to watch by looking through the *Radio Times* or the Sky planner and selecting thoughtfully and prayerfully.

The decisions we make when we plan our TV watching have a significant effect upon us and our relationships with God, with others, and with the world around – as do all the decisions we make about how we offer our bodies. What we do with our bodies is not irrelevant – it really matters. To explain why this is, we need to tell you a little about the danger of the Gnostic heresy and about the concept of praxis.

Mind, body and soul

Gnosticism is a broad religious and philosophical movement that particularly flourished in the first two centuries AD. It took many different forms and had many different consequences but the various branches of Gnosticism all contained the same common belief – that humans possess a good spirit which is held inside our bad physical bodies. The Gnostics believed that the spiritual and physical are completely separate entities; and consequently there was a type of Gnosticism which taught that we can do whatever we like with our bodies (which are inevitably bad anyway) since it will not affect our spirits (which are essentially good).

It is largely this type of Gnosticism which is still with us today. In particular there has been something of a

Gnostic revival in contemporary culture – due to the archaeological discoveries of Gnostic writings (found at Nag Hammadi, in Egypt, in December 1945) and the teachings of philosophers and psychologists such as Carl Jung (who viewed the Gnostic philosophy as a key to psychological interpretation and as vastly superior to orthodox Christianity).

Tragically we see the effects of this with some Christians who seem to think that their faith and their lifestyle are completely separate issues. A young Christian leader, working with UCCF,[3] recently told how many Christian students could see no conflict between their professed faith in Christ (which they sought to demonstrate through enthusiastic participation in praise celebrations) and their lifestyle (shown by the way they would get drunk and be sexually promiscuous). They think they can lead two completely separate lives which won't affect each other. This will always lead to problems – rather like those faced by the character Gary Sparrow in the BBC TV series *Goodnight Sweetheart*. Gary stumbles on a time portal which takes him back to London in the 1940s, where he falls in love with a barmaid called Phoebe. Rather than choose between Phoebe or his modern-day wife Yvonne, Gary decides to maintain two separate lives some 50 years apart, shuttling backwards and forwards between the two times and the two women, enduring any number of complications in the process. We have one life, and every part of it interacts with every other part. We simply aren't designed to detach and compartmentalise like this.

The Bible warned against the influence of such dualistic ideas. Indeed some scholars believe that a number of the letters in the New Testament were written, at least in part, to deal with the Gnostic heresy that was seeking to pervert the Christian gospel. The Bible makes it clear that the physical and the spiritual are both created good by God, and are intimately connected. What we do physically affects us spiritually, and vice versa. Paul makes this very clear in his letter to the church at Corinth when he says, 'Do you not know that your bodies are members of Christ himself? . . . Therefore honour God with your body' (1 Corinthians 6:15–20).

Peak praxis

What we do with our body does affect us spiritually. It affects our understanding of ourselves and our relationship with God; it affects the way we think and the way we feel. In another context, this type of process has been recognised by many educationalists, who often refer to the concept of praxis.

In educational theory, praxis is the idea that people learn through action (what they do) as well as through words (what they hear or read). This theory has a long history, with roots in the thinking and practice of Aristotle.[4] It was developed by Karl Marx with his emphasis on critical-practical activity (although this has been interpreted in different ways[5]), and it is used by many today who seek to help people to learn through activity.

Putting it another way, we all know that what we think and feel affects what we say and do. The concept of praxis points out that what we say and do also affects what we think and feel. Thus, what we do with our body is very important – it will affect our mind and our spirit.

This was illustrated recently in an episode of the BBC series *Spooks*. MI5 agent Zoë was working undercover, posing as a teacher at a secondary school. Her fictitious role as a teacher was only to provide cover for her real role as an agent. However, the longer she spent in that school environment, the more affection she developed for the pupils. Gradually, she spent more time talking with them and helping them. Soon, although she didn't need to, she was staying up late at night preparing lessons and marking their work. This tough spy-catcher was developing the heart and mind of a teacher through doing the work of a teacher – what she said and did had affected what she thought and felt.

In the same way, spending time with the TV will tend to have an affect upon what the viewer thinks and feels. For example, if you watch programmes that make light of people's suffering you will find that this affects your empathy, and if you watch programmes that glorify the accumulation of personal wealth you will find that this affects your generosity. So we need to be very careful about how we watch TV – in the same way that we must be careful about how we 'offer our bodies' in every other aspect of life.

Giving over, not giving up

Romans 12:1 tells us that we are to offer our bodies 'as living sacrifices'. These concepts of 'living' and 'sacrifice' are major themes in the Bible and can tell us a lot about how Christians should watch TV. Let's look first at the idea of sacrifice in scripture, where we will see how this is not so much about 'giving up' (as the term is often used in contemporary culture) but more about 'giving over'. That is, it is about a complete transformation of our hearts and minds as well as our actions. Then we will look at how the idea of living is presented in scripture. We will see how this is not about going with the flow, but nor is it about pushing the boundaries and living on the edge. Rather, it is about the satisfying and fulfilling life that God intends for us to experience as we live in his world his way.

Generally, in our culture, when we come across the concept of sacrifice it refers to someone giving up something, and this is usually in order to obtain something else. For example, in *Celebrity Fit Club* we watch the participating celebrities' anguish as they give up their favourite food and drink in pursuit of their desired weight loss. This is a secular version of a religious approach to sacrifice which seems to have been with humans throughout history. Anthropologists tell us that in every race, the earliest record of their activity shows that they 'offered sacrifices' to their deity in order to obtain favours or to avoid disaster.

The Bible's concept of sacrifice is different to this in a number of ways – here are two of them.

First, according to the Bible, sacrifice is not something that humans do to earn favour with God. Indeed the first and the last sacrifices in the Bible are both carried out by God himself for us. They show him giving us his undeserved favour, what the Bible calls 'grace'. In the Garden of Eden, God responds to Adam and Eve's sin by making them clothes from animal skins (Genesis 3:21). This is a process that will have required the death of the animals and thus one which theologians point to as the first sacrifice for sin. Then, in Jesus, God demonstrates his grace (his undeserved favour) to us by giving his own son as the final, ultimate, sacrifice for our sins. The writer to the Hebrews puts it this way, 'we have been made holy through the sacrifice of the body of Jesus Christ once for all (Hebrews 10:10).' So in these examples sacrifice demonstrates God's grace to us. He shows his loving care for us and he provides a way for us to come into a right relationship with him.

Secondly, when God told his people to sacrifice their animals, this was not to be an external religious action earning spiritual brownie points, but rather an outward and physical expression of an inward and spiritual response. We see this many times in between the first and last sacrifices in the Bible. That is why King Saul is told, 'Does the Lord delight in burnt offerings and sacrifices as much as in obeying the voice of the Lord? To obey is better than sacrifice' (1 Samuel 15:22). And, later, God says through the prophet Hosea, 'for I desire mercy, not sacrifice, and acknowledgment of God rather than burnt offerings' (Hosea 6:6).

These two aspects of sacrifice are important to keep in mind when we think what it means for our bodies to be a living sacrifice in relation to our TV watching.

First, this is not a call to us to give up watching certain TV shows in order to earn God's favour. This is a call to us to recognise how much he loves us and how he wants us to live in a relationship with him through everything we do – including our TV watching. As with every part of our lives, our TV watching should build our relationship with God. If it doesn't, if it damages our relationship with him because of the programmes we are watching or the way in which we are watching them, then we should stop doing it. But, when we do so, this is not to earn favour with God. It is because we value his grace to us and the relationship with him that he has made possible for us.

Secondly, this is not a call to us to try to fool God into being impressed with us by turning off certain programmes when we are really still watching them in our hearts. Offering our bodies as living sacrifices is not meant to be an attempt at the spiritual equivalent of *Faking It*. In this programme someone learns how to perform out of character – perhaps a vicar becomes a used car salesman or a ballet dancer becomes a wrestler. The question is – have they learned to fake it so well that they can fool a panel of experts? We can never fake it with God, he sees into our hearts and minds.[6] And it is those hearts and minds that he wants to transform by his Spirit, so that we will want our TV watching to be something that enables us to grow more like Jesus. That is why we are better to think about sacrifice in terms of 'giving over' rather than 'giving up'. It is about living a full and fulfilled life in a relationship with God, with our hearts and minds transformed by him.

This is the life that Jesus meant when he said 'I have come that they may have life and have it to the full (John 10:10).' This is the life that is referred to in the phrase 'living sacrifices'. We are not dead sacrifices for whom all life has gone, nor even unconscious ones who are not capable of making choices – we are living sacrifices, living life to the full.

Away from the edge

Shortly we will look at what this means. But first let's look at what it doesn't mean. It doesn't mean the kind of life that is often portrayed on TV and lived in our culture. That is a life that is going with the flow or a life that is pushing the boundaries and living on the edge.

In our culture there are many forces acting on us, leading us to live in a certain way. Some of these come from inside – they are in our human nature; some come from outside – they are in the culture that is around us. Psychologists will sometimes talk about these as an internal or external locus of control. There are a number of places in which these internal and external forces come together, and one of these is on the TV screen. As the number of TV channels expands, so their competition for ratings intensifies. One of the ways in which they compete is by offering programmes that appeal to viewers. That is, they are delivered externally (on the TV screen) because they appeal to our internal desires (in our human nature). So, if we watch TV without carefully assessing what we watch, we will find ourselves going with the flow of our human nature, reinforced by the TV producers who want to appeal to that human nature.

The Bible makes it clear that our human nature is not how God intended it to be. When we turned our backs on God (historically in Adam and Eve, but continually in each of our lives since then), our human nature became corrupted. Theologians call this the fall. It is not that we have a completely different nature, but rather one which has been somehow twisted. Take love for example. We were created to love, but our loving nature has become corrupted by the fall and as a result we tend to love ourselves. A natural ability to love others has become a natural tendency to self-centred self-love.

That is why much of TV encourages us to love ourselves – this is the kind of 'living' that we naturally find attractive. This is particularly evident in TV adverts, which are not only competing (against the kettle or the toilet) for our attention, but also competing for the pound in our pocket. So they tell us that we should buy a particular shampoo 'because you're worth it'. Or we should buy a particular chocolate bar because your 'happiness' wants it.

Our fallen nature wants pleasure, but it also wants excitement and to try out new things, particularly if there is an element of danger and excitement about them. As well as leading us to live a life which goes with the flow, TV often also invites us out onto the edge. Whereas Jesus gave us a prayer that said 'lead me not into temptation', our TV screens say 'lead me into temptation'.

Pushing back the boundaries

In January 2005, the BBC ignored the campaign of protest from Christians and broadcast *Jerry Springer: The Opera* as part of its *Jerry Springer Night*. The show's artistic director admitted the show was a deliberate attack on good taste, and the BBC conceded that the broadcast 'pushes back the boundaries of taste and decency'. That is a phrase that has become very familiar in the media in recent years. A biblical perspective on boundaries is that they are a good thing – they are given to protect us from harm, in the same way that parents put a fireguard around a fire to protect their children. But many in the media promote 'pushing the boundaries' as a good thing – something which validates art. Thus we are told that something is good art because it pushes the boundaries. That is not a biblical perspective on good art. The Bible shows us that good art is art that reflects the creativity of God who is the creator – not the corruption of the devil who is the destroyer.

So the Bible calls us to a life which is neither following temptation by pushing boundaries, nor is it merely going with the flow of our fallen nature. Rather it is living life in the way that God created us to live – in a right relationship with him, with ourselves, with other people and with the world.

This isn't easy. And it is particularly difficult if we allow our TV watching to be a powerful force that influences us. If we are going to avoid that, we need to make sure that God is Lord not just of our lives, and make sure that we know how to please him with our TV viewing. Which is what we will be talking about in the next chapter.

Study questions:

'So, we have a choice – we can offer our bodies to sin, which the Bible warns us against; or offer them to God, which the Bible encourages us to do.' How do you react to this statement?

How does our culture encourage us to use our bodies? How is this reflected in TV? How does that differ from what the Bible teaches us?

How do you currently decide what TV shows you will watch? Is that a good method? Why?

Which TV shows (or types of show) present you with the most temptation to sin? How do you deal with this temptation?

Do you think that your current TV watching builds or damages your relationship with God?

Notes

1 *Empire* magazine March 2004. Five years previously *Empire* readers voted it as their number 20.
2 This is an example of a common popular theological misconception. Clarence is a human who died several centuries previously who has become an angel, whereas in the Bible angels are spiritual creatures who were created as angels, not humans who have gained promotion.
3 The Universities and Colleges Christian Fellowship is an excellent Christian ministry seeking to help University students (see www.uccf.org.uk).
4 See *Nicomachean Ethics* by Aristotle (written 350 BC, translated by W. D. Ross). Available for download at http://classics.mit.edu/Aristotle/nicomachaen.html
5 See, for example, *Towards the Understanding of Karl Marx : A Revolutionary Interpretation*, by Sidney Hook, Ernest B. Hook, Paul Berman, Lewis S. Feuer, Christopher Phelps (Prometheus Books, 2002).
6 Man looks at the outward appearance, but the LORD looks at the heart (1 Samuel 16:7).

3

Food and Drink in *Babylon 5*
What Does it Mean to be Holy and Pleasing to God?

Therefore, I urge you brothers [and sisters], in view of God's mercy, to offer your bodies as living sacrifices, holy and pleasing to God – which is your spiritual worship. Do not conform any longer to the pattern of this world, but be transformed by the renewing of your mind. Then you will be able to test what God's will is – his good, pleasing and perfect will.

Romans 12:1–2

Most Christians have an idea that holiness means something about being separate or different. Does this mean that we should be the Christian equivalent of David Blaine? In 2003, for a TV stunt, he locked himself in a box suspended in the air above London for 44 days – thus separating himself completely from this culture, including its TV (although paradoxically, his every movement was captured live by TV cameras and watched with interest by TV viewers around the world).

Is holiness like this – complete separation from the

world? If so, why is the centre of the Bible the incarnation – in which the holy God was born into this world and lived among us?

What it means to be holy is a question that all Christians must consider as we live in this TV dominated culture. Can we be holy and please God through our TV watching? Or does that mean that we must reject all of TV? One Christian speaker back in the 1970s made it quite clear that he thought that TV and holiness could not go together. He frequently told the story of when he bought a TV, and then immediately sent it back when he read the advertising slogan on the box . . . 'bring the world into your home'. For him, the world was inherently evil and to be shunned – if the TV brought the world into his home then he didn't want anything to do with it!

We have a great deal of sympathy with his view. There are many programmes on TV that we simply do not want in our home. Anyone with Sky will know that this service brings many good channels (including the excellent channel 884 – UCB Bible – which broadcasts the Bible read very clearly and dramatically 24hrs a day). But it also carries many dreadful channels – just a button away. If you operate the Sky planner using the remote control, the first channel you are offered is BBC1, if you scroll downwards you move through BBC2, ITV etc, but if you scroll upwards you are immediately into the pornographic channels – from Playboy TV to XplicitXXX (thankfully, one cannot access these without payment via a pin-number – but, more worryingly, in the evening they offer 'free samples' for anyone to watch).

Bending to Babylon

So how do we deal with this mixture of good and bad on TV? How do we select the good and reject the bad? How do we watch TV and yet be holy and pleasing to God?

This is not a new problem. It is one that has been faced by missionaries for many years. Traditionally, when a missionary moved to another country, they found themselves immersed in a culture that was both good and bad. In particular, there were elements of that culture that the missionary had to carefully consider in order to decide whether to stand against them for the sake of holiness, or accept them as a harmless aspect of this different culture. For example, a British missionary moving to some places in Africa might find that the men did not wear suits and the women did not wear dresses – that clearly was just a cultural difference. But what about the women being topless – is that just a cultural difference or is it something which they should stand against? What about the practice of polygamy – is that just cultural? What about female genital excision – should they try to stop that or just accept it? And so the list goes on.

Part of the challenge for missionaries, living in another culture, has always been to discern what to accept and what to reject – how to be holy and pleasing to God in that culture. Now, all Christians living in our TV dominated world face the same challenge (but usually without the same support and training that we have provided for our missionaries in the past). What do we accept and what do we reject on TV? What is simply a cultural expression which we may or may not like, and what is ungodly, idolatrous, unholy programming that we should actively oppose? In short, how can we be holy and pleasing to God with the remote control in our hands?

To help us to consider this question, let's go back even further than the missionaries. Let's look right back to an example in the Bible. There we will find people who faced a similar dilemma and we can see how they resolved it. We will look at the example of Daniel and his three friends in the Old Testament.

Many Christians will be familiar with the story of Daniel and how he stood up in a hostile culture. What is quite clear is that Daniel and his friends would not compromise on holiness. They were determined to stand out for God – whatever it cost them.

So, we see Daniel refusing to give up praying to God – even though this meant that he would face the death penalty. With his windows open towards Jerusalem he got down on his knees and prayed openly three times a day (Daniel 6:10). No matter what the people around him did, he would not compromise. He would pray to God and him alone – even if it meant that he would be thrown into the lions' den to be eaten alive (Daniel 6:12).

And we see Daniel's friends refusing to bow down to a golden statue – even though this meant that they would face the death penalty. When the music played and everyone else bowed down to worship the image, they refused (Daniel 3:12). Whatever anyone else did, they would not compromise. They would worship God and him alone – even if it meant that they would be thrown into the fiery furnace to be burned alive (Daniel 3:15).

Similarly, Daniel and his friends together refused to eat food from the king's table because they didn't want to defile themselves (Daniel 1:8). They would not compromise on holiness. Wherever they were, whatever they were doing, and however anyone else behaved around them, they would stand out for God.

If Daniel and his friends were alive today we don't know exactly how they would react to TV. But we can be sure that they would do nothing with the remote control that would compromise their holiness before God. So, from this story we may take courage and strength to stand for God in our TV culture.

Standing firm

Many of us are attracted to the idea of taking a stand. Rather like in the episode of *Friends* where Ross discovered a pornographic video which apparently had Phoebe acting in it (actually it was her twin sister). Joey, although an avid fan of porn, refused to watch it because he thought it featured his friend. While the others took their places around the TV, Joey made a stand and refused to watch.

However, when we take a stand we must make sure that we are standing in the right place. If we reject certain TV shows and accept others because we want to be holy and pleasing to God, then we must make sure that we understand what God requires of us.

That is why we need to consider the whole story of Daniel. We may be used to the stories we have recounted above, but we may be surprised to realise that Daniel and his friends were willing to accept other aspects of their godless culture. They accepted their education. They accepted their jobs. They even accepted their new names.[1] When we look at these more closely we might be surprised by these actions. And this may give us cause to think more deeply about what we accept and reject on TV.

So let's look carefully at the story of Daniel. It is set around 600 BC. The country of Assyria had ruled the Middle East for some 150 years, their strong military rule had taken over many small nations and had smashed and scattered Israel. Judah had been spared, but as little more than a small satellite country of Assyria. Now, times were changing. Assyria was collapsing, and Babylon, with its young king Nebuchadnezzar, was the rising power in the region (in fact Babylon became the dominant power for the next 70 years). At the beginning of the book of Daniel, we find that Nebuchadnezzar had come to Jerusalem and besieged it (Daniel 1:1).

When he captured the city he plundered articles from God's temple and took them back into his pagan temple in Babylonia (Daniel 1:2). In addition to this he also took back to Babylon some of the royal family and the nobility of Israel. They were possibly taken as hostages to ensure that Judah would now obey his commands. Almost certainly they were taken to be brainwashed and sent back to Jerusalem as loyal servants of Babylon – a strategy that would ensure the king's ongoing control of these conquered people. Amongst this group of hostages were Daniel and his three friends (Daniel 1:6).

They were probably just teenagers. Almost certainly they were training for religious and government service in Jerusalem. They were being prepared to serve God in the city of David – but now they find themselves torn away and dumped in a pagan land full of idols.

This is rather like the popular TV series *Quantum Leap*, in which the unfortunate scientist Sam Beckett repeatedly finds himself leaping into someone else's body in another part of the world, in another moment in time. There, he must live their life, and put right something that had gone wrong, hoping that he would then leap back to his own life in his own part of the world at his own time. Daniel and his friends knew that, in a strange and foreign land, they must do what is right. But they would only be going home when God's prophecy was fulfilled and the nation in which they now lived was removed from power.

So here we have God's people in a hostile culture. How do they react? We know that they take a stand against the idol worship, against the food from the kings table, and for open prayer to God. But what do they also accept in this culture?

Exiles excel

First of all, we see that they accept their new pagan education. In Jerusalem they would have learned the story of God's creation; the history of Abraham and the Patriarchs; they would have learned the law and the prophets.[2] Now, in this pagan land they learn 'the language and literature of the Babylonians' (Daniel 1:4).

In the material that they learned, there would have been some parts that were consistent with their faith in God. They will probably have learned some maths, some astronomy, and even some early form of science.[3] It seems unlikely that Daniel and his friends would have become involved in some of the more occult practices that their Babylonian peers studied, but we are told of the exiled Israelites that 'In every matter of wisdom and under-standing about which the king questioned them, he found them ten times better than all the magicians and enchanters in his whole kingdom' (Daniel 1:20). Daniel himself eventually became the chief of all the astrologers, magicians, enchanters and diviners. This does not necessarily mean that Daniel practised such things himself: the incidents of Daniel's life which the Bible tells us about suggest that throughout his service in Babylon, Daniel made his dependence on God (as opposed to occult practices) very clear.

We have to be careful whenever we seek to learn lessons today from the particular experience of biblical characters in the past. But it does seem that if we, today, want to be like Daniel we should not necessarily reject the current TV, films and music. If Daniel was prepared to study the culture of his day, ought we also to be prepared to study the culture of our day?

To serve them all my days

Secondly, we see that Daniel accepts his new job. He is not only there studying the language and literature of the Babylonians; he is also actively engaged in that culture, as he 'entered the king's service' (Daniel 1:19). We don't know exactly what he did in his work but he clearly had some kind of role in the government service.

Here is this young man, who had been training and preparing to serve God and his people in Jerusalem, but he is now serving a pagan king in an idolatrous country. And he would know, from his knowledge of the prophets, that this country which he is now serving is in fact under the judgement of God and will not last. Yet he works in and for it. He doesn't just study it; he becomes a part of it.

If Daniel were in our culture today, he would clearly work with diligence and integrity. Perhaps he would be working in the civil service (and would be as efficient as Sir Humphrey was in the BBC series *Yes Minister*, though certainly with more integrity). Or perhaps he would be working in television? Certainly we cannot simply assume that he would automatically refuse a media job simply because that media is a channel for so much ungodliness.

My name is

Thirdly, he accepts a new name – and so do his three friends. So Daniel becomes Belteshazzar, Hananiah becomes Shadrach, Mishael becomes Meshach, and Azariah becomes Abednego. These were significant changes. To those people at that time names were very important. This was particularly so for Daniel and his three friends, since their names contained the name of God – the suffixes 'el' and 'iah' were names for God. But when they were given new names, these were based on the names of the Babylonian gods, whom they knew to be pagan idols.[4]

So here are these young men who are not only prepared to learn the language and literature of the Babylonians, and to work in the service of Babylon, but also to be known by names based upon the pagan idols of the time.

Today, names are not so significant for us. However, we do use the phrase 'making a name for herself'. Our reputation is important. As Christians we want to be known for our holiness and service to God. However, if we are to follow the example of Daniel and his friends, perhaps we might be prepared to accept other reputations as well – even reputations which, on the face of it, may appear to be acknowledging elements of an ungodly culture?

Exclusive covenant

So Daniel and his three friends accept these three changes. In these particular areas, they fit in with the culture – even though it must have been very painful for them. This is rather like the episode from the popular children's cartoon series *SpongeBob SquarePants*, in which

Bob leaves his 'pineapple under the sea' and goes to live
with the jellyfish. He has to fit in, he has to adapt to
sleeping on the floor and eating different food – but it is
painful for him.

Now, given the story so far, you may be wondering
why Daniel objected to the food. We can see why he
objected to the ban on prayer. We can see why his friends
objected to the requirement to worship the golden statue.
But, if they were prepared to learn the Babylonian
language and literature, to work in their service and even
to accept a name based on their idols – why on earth
wouldn't they eat the food? Why does it say, 'Daniel
resolved not to defile himself with the royal food and
wine' (Daniel 1:8)?

Some people have suggested that this was because the
food was 'unclean' in terms of the Jewish laws about diet.
But, others have pointed out that if this were the reason,
then it would not explain why Daniel rejects the wine –
since there is no prohibition placed on wine. Others have
argued that this food must have been sacrificed to idols.
But, still others have pointed out that if this were true,
then it would not explain why it was alright for them to
eat the vegetables and water.[5]

The explanation for the rejection of the food that makes
most sense to many scholars is centred on verse 5, which
says 'The king assigned them a daily amount of food and
wine from the king's table.' The food they were offered
wasn't just any old food, it wasn't even just food that was
really special. It was food that came from the king's table
and it was given to them by the king. Such an action held
a huge significance in that culture at that time. When a
king gave you food to eat from his table, eating it
established a covenant bond between you – like a
contract, an unbreakable agreement.

If Daniel had done this, it would have been far more

intense than just learning some information, or doing some work, or being called by another name. He would have been accepting a specific bond and relationship of commitment to the king. When people ate food given by the king from his table, they were accepting a covenant bond with him.

So it seems that this is why Daniel and his friends asked not to eat the food. His bond, his commitment, his covenant relationship was with God, and with God alone. And being holy meant being wholly committed to God – not letting anything come in the way of that.

So, if Daniel were here in this culture today, we might not be surprised to see him watch the films and read the books and listen to the music. He might be prepared to engage with the media and work in it. He might even accept a reputation for his work in the media. But we can be sure that he wouldn't do anything that would establish a bond with ungodly things that would damage his covenant bond with God.

And that is what it means to be holy – to be set apart in our hearts for God, and to let nothing take the place of that bond which we have with him. And that is what we will then want to apply to our TV watching. Whilst there is nothing intrinsically wrong with watching TV, or studying TV, or being involved in TV production, or even developing a reputation for one's knowledge and involvement in TV, we will want to ensure that we do nothing that damages our covenant relationship with God.

TV listings

What would be great now would be to close this particular chapter with a simple list of TV programmes that are the equivalent of what Daniel accepted and a list that are the equivalent of what he rejected. Then we could all very easily be holy and pleasing to God with the remote in our hands. We would know what to watch and what to avoid. However, that isn't possible. The difficulty doesn't just come from the fact that there are so many programmes. It comes from the fact that it is not just the nature of the programme that makes it good or bad for us to watch. It is also the way in which we watch it and particularly how it affects us and others around us. And that, in turn, is dependent upon what it means to us.

This issue of our individual response is what we will pick up in the next chapter when we consider how being holy and pleasing to God is our spiritual act of worship. When we look at holiness through the eyes of worship we will see how each of us needs to develop our own spiritual wisdom and understanding so that we can each know what we should and shouldn't watch – and how we should watch when we do.

Of course that is harder to do than just looking up a list of good and bad programmes. It would be so much easier to have a simple list – but that isn't possible because we are such complex creatures and our interaction with TV is even more complex. So we have to think and pray and consider more deeply. That's what we will continue with in the next chapter – don't go away.

Study questions:

What lessons can you learn from the way that Daniel interacted with the Babylonian culture? How should you apply those lessons to our very different cultural situation?

Why is it so important to engage with our TV dominated culture?

To what extent does being holy and pleasing to God affect your decisions about what to watch on TV?

Think about the programmes you have watched in the last month. Do any aspects of your TV viewing bind you to ungodly things and affect your relationship with God?

Notes

1 It could be argued that Daniel and his friends had little choice in accepting their names. But there are other issues which they have taken a stand on, even to the point of being sentenced to death, so at the very least, the issue of names is one that they acquiesced to.
2 At least some of the early ones.
3 The term 'language and literature' was a short hand term covering a wide range of scholarship at that time.
4 Some scholars say these refer to pagan gods Shack and Nego, but others say that we don't know which pagan gods are referred to since the names that have been written in the book of Daniel were deliberately corrupted because they refer to pagan gods.
5 The vegetables would not have been offered to idols in the same sacrificial way that the animals were – but there would have been some cultic ritual associated with their planting and growth.

4

Sacrificed to *Pop Idol*
What is Our Spiritual Act of Worship

> Therefore, I urge you brothers [and sisters], in view
> of God's mercy, to offer your bodies as living
> sacrifices, holy and pleasing to God – which is your
> spiritual worship. Do not conform any longer to the
> pattern of this world, but be transformed by the
> renewing of your mind. Then you will be able to test
> what God's will is – his good, pleasing and perfect
> will.
>
> **Romans 12:1–2**

When we think of worship, our minds may go to sitting
with Grandma watching *Songs of Praise*, or *My Favourite
Hymns*. Is that what worship is? Or is it dancing with
thousands of others in a tent filled with the sound of the
latest worship band? Or is it some quiet liturgy in a
country church? And, in addition to all of these
questions, can our TV watching be part of our worship?

To answer any such questions we must begin with the
Bible – what does that tell us? There are two major
aspects of worship that we see in the Bible and these are
both particularly relevant to us as we consider what it
means to worship God in our TV watching. The first is

the concept of glorifying God, and the second is the concept of serving him.

When we glorify God in our worship we recognise his glory and respond to it. The Bible tells us that there is only one God and he, uniquely, has eternal power and divine nature. This is his glory. He shows this through his creation (Romans 1:20), through his actions (Isaiah 44:23), and through his Son (John 17:5). Our response to God's glory is to glorify him. Theologians call this 'doxology', which means proclaiming his ultimate greatness. This is a major aspect of Christian worship and the Bible gives us many examples.[1]

When we serve God in our worship we recognise that he is our Lord and master and we respond to him in humble submission. In the Bible, two common words used for worship (*ebed* in Hebrew and *latreia* in Greek) both literally mean 'service' and were originally used to refer to the labour of slaves or hired servants. So, Christian worship is not just what we do with our voices as we glorify God – it is also what we do with our lives as we serve him.

Taking these two aspects of worship together we can see why the Bible commands us to 'have no other gods' (Exodus 20:3) and to 'love the LORD your God with all your heart and with all your soul and with all your strength and with all your mind' (Luke 10:27). Worship which is glorifying God and serving him is only possible if we are worshipping one unique God. We can only proclaim the ultimate greatness of one God. It is simply impossible for more than one to be the greatest. And we can only serve one master, it is simply impossible for us to have two masters.

So, worship is about recognising the uniqueness of God – by proclaiming his ultimate greatness and by serving him alone.

We live in a world in which there are many things that

can seek to take God's place. There are many objects of desire that can become the centre of our attention and many powerful forces that can control us. Most of these are not bad in themselves, but when they interact with us they can become a problem.

Remote control

Celebrity is one example of something that can become the centre of our attention. The success of shows such as *Pop Idol* and *Big Brother* depend upon the desire that many people have to become celebrities. There is nothing wrong with celebrities in themselves. They are individuals created in the image of God. But, because of the way they are portrayed in the media, they can become the focus of our adoration. We can long to become like them, rather than like God. We can look to them for inspiration and guidance, rather than to God.

Similarly, alcohol is an example of one thing that can become a controlling factor in our lives. There is nothing wrong with alcohol in itself. The Bible says that God gave it to us to 'gladden the heart of man' (Psalm 104:15), and Jesus created huge amounts of it in his first miracle (John 2:1–11). But alcohol can become our master. Many alcoholics will talk about their path into alcoholism in terms of a shift from 'using alcohol' to 'being used by alcohol'. That is, they became alcoholic when they could no longer control alcohol, but the alcohol controlled them.

Now, TV is rather like both of these. It can become the centre of our attention and the locus of our control. There is nothing wrong with TV in itself. It can be something that we can appreciate as one of the results of the creativity that God has given those who invented and developed it. It can also be a means by which we can view and appreciate the creativity of TV producers, directors and actors. But it is possible for it to become the object of our worship.

It can become the centre of our lives – just as it has become the centre of many lounges. In the same way that many rooms have all the chairs facing the TV screen, so we can have all our thoughts turning towards it. Thus, like the celebrity-fan, we find ourselves constantly thinking about the TV programmes and focusing our attention on them.

Similarly, it can become something that controls us. We can find ourselves unable to resist turning it on. So we watch whatever is on without any real discernment, and then we find ourselves unable to turn it off. Thus, like the alcoholic, we have become telly-addicts.

This was illustrated recently in a comic moment in the sitcom *My Family*. Someone asked dippy son Nick if he was free at a certain time on a certain day. 'Wait a moment' he replied, 'let me consult my diary.' And, in a movement that probably amused many viewers because it was so close to the truth in their lives, he picked up the *Radio Times* to see if he would be busy then.

Paul refers to this sort of distinction in his letter to the Corinthians when he says, 'everything is permissible for me, but I will not be mastered by anything' (1 Corinthians 6:12). If he were writing today, no doubt he would tell people that 'TV is permissible for me, but I will not be mastered by it'. For Paul the remote control must be something that we use to control the TV, not something that the TV uses to control us.

Paul actually repeats this little phrase, 'everything is permissible for me, but. . .' in two places in this letter. In chapter 6 he considers it in relation to sex and food. Then, again, in chapter 10, he considers it in relation to food that had been sacrificed to idols. And it is here, in this latter case (1 Corinthians 10:23–33), that we can particularly get some help in understanding how, although TV can be a good thing as part of our worship of God, it can become a bad thing which damages us and others around us.

So we will now spend some time in this passage, considering what it meant in that place at that time – and seeing if we can discover some general principles that we can apply to our situation of TV watching here and now.

Can't eat won't eat

At the time when Paul was writing, the process of animal sacrifice was part of the whole social, commercial and domestic life of the community. After an animal was sacrificed in a temple, a small amount of the meat was 'offered' to the idol, and then the rest was eaten at a cultic meal at the temple. This was an integral part of the community life. Indeed, if you were a member of some particular trades or professions, you were expected to attend these meals. Furthermore, some of the pagan temples put on free meals for the poor – who were able to sit at the table in the idol's temple and eat food that they could not possibly afford to buy for themselves.

But, some of the meat that had been sacrificed in the temples was surplus to these requirements. This was passed on from the temple officials to the meat dealers who sold it at the market. Shoppers buying food for their family would particularly look out for this meat since it was the best food (because the animal for sacrifice must be perfect, and without blemish). When this meat was taken home it was eaten without ceremony – but the host might (presumably to show off how good the meat was) point out that this food had come from a sacrifice at a temple.

Now we can see why the question of 'food sacrificed to idols' was such an issue to the young Christians at Corinth. They were surrounded by it. It was part of their family, commercial and community life. Rather like TV today, they couldn't get away from it – everywhere they turned, there it was. If they were poor (and it seems there were many amongst the Christians in Corinth[2]) then they were probably used to 'eating in an idol's temple' (1 Corinthians 8:10) to make ends meet. If they were rich, then they were probably used to buying the good (sacrificial) meat at the market. If they were in a trade or profession then they probably were expected to attend meals at the temples. If they had friends then they probably were given sacrificial meat by their generous hosts. Rather like a street today, where every house has a TV aerial or a satellite dish, at that time every house would have some involvement in meat that had been sacrificed to idols.

This is rather like the episode of *Blackadder* when Sir Francis Drake was coming back to Britain. Blackadder didn't want to be involved in the celebrations, but everywhere he looked there were people shouting, singing and wearing silly hats. Even locking himself away in his room didn't cut him off from it, because the noise of cheering came through the window, and his friends came through the door (wearing silly hats). There are things in our culture that we just can't seem to get away from no matter what we do. TV is one of those and so, like Blackadder, we have to face up to it.

So Paul addresses this question for them – and he does it in some detail. In chapter 8 he considers the question of food that is eaten at the temple. Then in chapter 10 he looks at food that is sold in the meat market. When we take these together we can see that, in both cases, he guides them by identifying five general principles. And we can see that all of these can, with appropriate care, be applied to our world of TV.

Five principles

First of all, he points out that there is no power in the meat itself. It doesn't contain any magical properties, even if it has been sacrificed to an idol. Paul points out that 'an idol is nothing at all' (1 Corinthians 8:4), these are not real gods, they are just statues and images. They don't have the power that God has. And food is just food, whoever it has been sacrificed to – even if it had been sacrificed to God himself 'food does not bring us near to God; we are no worse if we do not eat, and no better if we do' (1 Coritnhians 8:8). So they have no reason to worry about the actual food itself.

Secondly, he highlights the freedom that they have in Christ. This is a subject that he stresses in many of his letters, and it seems to have been a particular problem for many Christians in the early church. He devotes much of Galatians to showing how Christians are not to rely upon following various laws – and sums it up with the great phrase 'It is for freedom that Christ has set us free' (Galatians 5:1). In Colossians he says, 'do not let anyone judge you by what you eat or drink' (Colossians 2:16). Here, in this passage he tells that they can 'eat anything sold in the meat market' (1 Corinthians 10:25), and he repeats the phrase we met earlier, 'everything is permissible' (1 Corinthians 10:23). However, this doesn't mean that they are free to eat in any way in any place, without regard to anyone else – since there are other important principles that must be taken into account, as we will see in the next two points Paul makes.

Thirdly, he warns them about the effect that exercising this freedom may have on them. He warns them that they shouldn't eat in a way that affects them – as part of the temple ceremony where 'the sacrifices of pagans are offered to demons' (1 Corinthians 10:20). He points out that 'you cannot drink the cup of the Lord and the cup of demons too' (1 Corinthians 10:21). What you do affects you. And 'those who eat the sacrifices participate in the altar' (1 Corinthians 10:18).

Fourthly, he warns them not to use their freedom in a way that will do damage to others. He says, 'Be careful, however, that the exercise of your freedom does not become a stumbling-block to the weak' (1 Corinthians 8:9). He reminds them that there are some people who are 'so accustomed to idols' (1 Corinthians 8:7) that they think of this food as being defiled. So, if they see another Christian eating it in a temple, they will think that this Christian must knowingly be doing something that is wrong. This then will reduce their sense of right and wrong. (Naturally, when they are tempted to do something which is wrong, they will remember seeing other people eating food sacrificed to idols. Even though they may be mistaken in regarding that as sinful, it will give them justification for giving in to their own temptation.) This is such a powerful danger that Paul even says, 'if what I eat causes my brother to fall into sin, I will never eat meat again' (1 Corinthians 8:13).

The fifth principle is implicit in each of the other four – but it is important to think it through carefully. Although there is nothing significant about the food itself, what is very significant is where, how and why they eat it. This is made particularly clear when Paul refers to the meat that has been bought from the meat market. He tells them that, if they are out for a meal with someone else, they should eat whatever is put before them without asking whether it had been sacrificed – that is, the meat itself is not significant. However, if someone says, 'this has been offered in sacrifice' (1 Corinthians 10:28) then don't eat it – the meat itself is no different, but it has now taken on significance in the mind of the person who said this.

TV times

So let's now see how we might apply these principles to our TV watching. But as we do that we will have to be careful to recognise that there is not a direct correspondence between TV and food sacrificed to idols. So let's be careful, but see what we can do.

First of all, rather like the meat in Paul's day, TV does not carry any magical power in itself. It simply delivers a set of changing pixels onto a screen. However, those pixels are recognised by our brains as images which have meaning. And those images carry with them certain underlying ideas and messages. Though the TV screen carries no significance or power, those ideas and messages do. They can shape our thoughts and beliefs, our actions and reactions. But the way in which they do that will depend upon how we look at them, what our motivation is, what is going on in our hearts and minds as we watch.

Secondly, Christ has set us free to enjoy the freedom that he has given us. We must not let ourselves be taken back into restrictions and rules that hold us captive. We must not let others judge us by what we watch or don't watch.

Thirdly, the TV that we watch will have an effect upon us. To paraphrase 1 Corinthians 10:21 'you cannot fill your hearts with God and fill your hearts with ungodly TV at the same time.' Certainly, no-one else is called to judge us for the TV we watch, but there is one who will judge us – one to whom we will have to give an account for our lives when we stand before him on the day of judgement. And that is God himself. Therefore, we must seek God's guidance about what we should watch or not watch. We must seek his direction about how we should watch and how we should respond to the TV that we do watch.

Fourthly, the programmes we watch will have an effect upon other people. We are not isolated individuals, we live in a community. The TV we watch will affect other people, whether we like it or not. The question we have to ask ourselves is this: will the TV we watch affect others in a way that leads them closer to God or further away from him? Like Paul, we must be prepared to say that we will not watch any TV if it 'causes my brother to fall into sin' (1 Corinthians 8:13).

Finally (and here is the most difficult principle to apply) we need to consider what each TV programme signifies to us and other people – and the effect that it has upon us and them. This will be different for different people. In the Damaris team there are those for whom any sexual image leads to thoughts which are profoundly unhelpful and deeply ungodly. Therefore, there are certain programmes that they will not watch. For others, the problem is with violent images.

Each of us needs to examine our own hearts and consider before God what we should or should not watch. And as we do so we must not just think about the TV programme itself, but what it means to us. What significance does this programme have to us? What thoughts does it evoke in our minds? What feelings does it stir up in our hearts? This will be different for different people at different times and in different places.

Thinking this way does not mean that we become moral relativists.[3] There are images and subjects that are absolutely wrong for all people in all places at all times.

And it is also absolutely wrong (for all people in all places at all times) for us to watch any programme in any way that leads us to put other thoughts and feelings in the place of God. However (and it is a very important however) different programmes will cause this problem for different people at different times. And the key factors are why and how you are watching.

Therefore, as we watch TV we must constantly seek to have in mind what it means to worship God – that is, to glorify him and to recognise him as our master. Then the programmes we choose to watch, and the way we choose to watch them, can celebrate the creativity of God and equip us to communicate his gospel in his world.

Mastermind

All of this requires us to develop a spiritual wisdom and understanding. It means that we must think deeply, not just at a superficial level, about the programmes and the effect they have upon us. For example, many programmes that seem fine on a surface level (e.g. there is no swearing or nudity or sexual scenes) are actually deeply damaging to people's relationship with God at a more fundamental level. And, conversely, some programmes which contain swearing, nudity or sex scenes can actually build people's relationship with God because of the message at a far deeper level (although we should still be very wary of the effect such images can have upon us and exercise caution in deciding whether or not to watch such programmes. It would be both easy and very wrong to use the 'deeper message' argument to justify watching things that we are really watching for sinful motives of titillation.)

So, in the next two chapters we will consider what it

means to think at this deeper level – by not conforming to the pattern of this world, and by being transformed by the renewing of our minds.

Study questions:

Think of a TV show which is likely to divide Christians – one where some will argue that it shouldn't be watched because of its content, and others will defend it because of a serious underlying message. What is your view on whether or not to watch this show?

How can you apply your understanding of 1 Corinthians 10 to the subject of watching TV?

Can you think of a time when you have allowed yourself to be controlled by your TV watching? What did you do about it? What should you do if you become aware of it happening again? How can you prevent it from happening?

Notes

1 Romans 11:33–36; Jude 24–25; and most of the Psalms!
2 See 1 Cor 1:26 and 1 Cor 11:22.
3 Moral relativism asserts that there is no absolute truth in morality. It claims that all right and wrong depends upon who you are, when you are, what you are, etc. Clearly very different from a biblical perspective on ethics.

5

The Waltons or *The Simpsons*? What Does it Mean to Not Conform to the Pattern of This World?

Therefore, I urge you brothers [and sisters], in view of God's mercy, to offer your bodies as living sacrifices, holy and pleasing to God – which is your spiritual worship. Do not conform any longer to the pattern of this world, but be transformed by the renewing of your mind. Then you will be able to test what God's will is – his good, pleasing and perfect will.

Romans 12:1–2

It was an interesting feud, all the more so for being so unevenly matched. It all started back in 1992 when George Bush senior, then the President of the United States of America, declared that the country needed to be 'closer to *The Waltons* than *The Simpsons*'.[1] *Simpsons'* creator Matt Groening declared war, and just two days later the opening titles of the show featured the family watching the President on TV. Bart addressed the camera and said, 'Hey, we're just like *The Waltons*. We're praying for an end to the depression too!'

As we said: a hopelessly uneven contest. The might

and power of the White House versus a humble animated comedy show. At the time, Bush's approval rating was running at a robust 90 per cent. Less than a year later, he lost the Presidential election to Bill Clinton. *The Simpsons* have continued to assert their superiority by sporadically making fun of ex-President Bush since then, including one episode where George and Barbara Bush move in across the street from the Simpson family. Some might say that it's a good thing that *The Simpsons* haven't tried anything similar with George W. Bush's Presidency yet, as his response might include invading the Fox Corporation, claiming it to be an enemy to democracy and that it was hoarding weapons of mass derision.

Although we don't necessarily accept Bush senior's assessment of *The Simpsons* as a bad role model for America, he does touch on an important point. Christians are expected to stand out from the world. Romans 12:2 warns us to 'not conform any longer to the pattern of this world'. Whatever Christians are meant to be, it is something recognisably distinct from what we find around us.

Television: mirror or mould?

The debate about whether television reflects society or shapes it has been around a long time. A friend of ours once claimed that his twelve-year-old daughter and her friends are unable to conduct a discussion in any way other than making a melodramatic speech and storming out of the room, because that is the only way of resolving conflict that TV soaps show them. We tried suggesting that there may be other causes, but our friend went into a lengthy monologue and swept out of the room!

Although what we see on television is, in many ways, a

reflection of what goes on in our society, TV also plays a part in shaping that society. It would be naïve to imagine that either of these statements is completely untrue. If we are serious about not being shaped by the prevailing values of the world, we need to learn how to identify those values and recognise whether they are compatible with getting more like Jesus.

For some shows, this is easier than others. It doesn't take a genius to work out the underlying messages behind the excellent cbeebies show *The Koala Brothers*, featuring the eponymous brothers Frank and Buster, who run an airstrip in the outback, and spend their days looking for people to help. With the catchphrase, 'We're here to help' and songs that encourage viewers to always help others, *The Koala Brothers* is typical of many children's shows in promoting positive moral values. Shows aimed at older viewers may not be so transparent, but that doesn't mean that they can't also reinforce a particular way of looking at the world.

Getting away with it

The long-running American comedy *Friends*[2] focuses on the lives and loves of a group of six twenty-somethings (at least, that's how old they were when *Friends* started) living in New York. Various crises are negotiated, and the show paints a picture of a generation who build supportive friendship-networks to take the place that family (or, indeed, church) filled for previous generations. The sense of loyalty that the show is built upon is reflected in numerous storylines from across the show's ten-year run. The glue that has held them together for all that time is their love and loyalty to one another over and above other bonds, and this kind of devoted, loving friendship is something that we would be wise not to dismiss.

On the other hand, almost every moral or ethical dilemma that is thrown at the six friends is dealt with according to the same criteria – what are the consequences? Put another way, 'Can I get away with this?' is asked far more often than 'Is this right or wrong?' In the episode *The One With The Giant Poking Device* (series 3) Ross' son Ben gets a bang on the head when Monica is looking after him. Monica's first response is to cover-up the accident in the hope that Ross never finds out, rather than telling him what had happened. Similarly, in *The One With The Apothecary Table*, (series 6) Rachel seeks to get around Phoebe's anti-consumerist principles by telling her that the apothecary table she bought from mass-production chain Pottery Barn was a bargain from a flea market. Rachel makes up an elaborate story of the table's provenance, and soon fills the flat with other so-called flea market bargains. When Rachel and Ross accidentally get married while drunk in Las Vegas (*The One Where Ross Hugs Rachel*, series 6), Ross baulks at having three divorces to his name, so he tells Rachel that his lawyer has sorted out an annulment, while in fact doing nothing to dissolve their legal status as husband and wife. Again and again the show presents us with a worldview that rejects the idea of absolute right and wrong, offering in its place a blurred vision of relative values and a narrowly situationalist approach to problem solving.

This is a problem because in reality we don't know what we can get away with, and we don't know the difference between an inconsequential misdeed that does no harm, and one which ruins lives or hurts people. The problem with judging ethics by the consequences of any given action is that we don't know all of the consequences. But God does, and that's why he has given us a moral framework for making decisions, to help us to tell right from wrong. Any such framework is absent from the world of *Friends*.

Community strife

In *EastEnders*, the inhabitants of Albert Square similarly show a sense of community, while also reflecting some of the less appealing facets of modern life. John Yorke, executive producer of *EastEnders*, has said that 'If *EastEnders* is about one thing, it's about . . . the Blitz Spirit, it's about however bad life gets, however terrible things are, you don't give in, you don't feel sorry for yourself, you fight back – you support those around you, you come together as a community and you shout from the roof tops, life IS worth living, it IS worth fighting for.'[3] Again and again, this sense of communal rallying round can be seen in the storylines on *EastEnders*: when Sonia dramatically went into labour (having not realised that she was even pregnant), the previously sour-tempered Mo Slater turned out to be a tower of strength, providing support and practical help right when it was needed. When the Ferreira family were evicted from their house, other residents stepped in to offer places to stay rather than see them left out on the street (the scriptwriters were less generous, just a few months later the entire family was axed from the show). In fact, there is much in the community life of *EastEnders* that mirrors the description of the early church in Acts 2:42–47 and Acts 4:32–37 (but without all the God stuff, obviously!).

But *EastEnders* repeatedly features major plot points that revolve around grudges, with the ruling principle seeming to be that of doing back to others at least as badly as they have done to you. A seemingly ever-

changing cast of small-time villains, from Phil Mitchell to
Andy Hunter; 'Dirty' Den Watts to Steve Owen, ensure
that tit-for-tat scheming is the order of the day. For
example, when Paul Truman was discovered to have
helped the police in an abortive attempt to arrest Andy
for drug trafficking, it was no surprise when Andy
arranged to have Paul killed. Even among residents who
generally stay on the right side of the law, revenge is a
common motivation. Ian Beale persecuted his then wife
Laura after she became pregnant with a baby that he
knew couldn't possibly be his.[4] After breaking up with
Laura, Ian devoted himself to ruining her life – making
unpleasant comments whenever they met, undermining
her attempts at making a living and generally doing
everything in his power to make her life miserable.

Ian is, even by the standards of *EastEnders*, a particularly petty little man. But even he has moments when
he rises above himself. It is true that not every character
in *EastEnders* is driven by revenge, and one of the
strengths of the show is the way that most of the
characters are, in time, developed and shown to have
many sides to their personalities. We see a range of three
dimensional characters, rather than single-issue stereotypes. Nevertheless, in the complex moral environment
of *EastEnders*, the oil that greases the wheel is a heady
mixture of revenge, scheming and deception.

Watching the worldviews

Those are just two examples of prevailing values in TV
shows, and Romans 12 happens to pick up on both of
them as things that Christians should avoid being
characterised by. Verse 9 tells us to 'hate evil' and 'cling to
what is good', rather than following the example of

Friends and clinging to what is convenient. Verses 19–20 tell us to show love and forgiveness to our enemies, rather than taking revenge. The point is that it is easy to watch a show without ever stopping to consider its prevailing moral assumptions. And if we aren't aware of those values, we are more vulnerable to find ourselves thinking in a similar way ourselves. If we want to avoid being shaped in the pattern of the world, we need to become better at recognising that pattern when we see it.

To help us, we need to apply a variation of the technique called positive deconstruction[5] to the shows we watch. We aren't trying to dismiss shows or to explain them away, and we aren't trying to spoil anyone's enjoyment. We don't have to agree philosophically with everything we watch, but we ought to be able to identify what the points of difference are.

Although some documentaries may represent a specific cohesive worldview, most TV programmes are more complex then that. A variety of characters will represent different ways of looking at the world, and different approaches to making decisions.

We need to take things one step at a time. When assessing any TV show for the worldview that it promotes, we need to recognise the different levels at which answers reveal themselves to us. At the most basic, there is the level of events – what is it that happens? What is it that is said? This is underpinned by the level of significance – what is the meaning of these things? What beliefs and values are expressed through them? Finally, the level of worldview – how do these ideas fit into a wider way of making sense of the world? Where do these beliefs come from? Is this consistent with a biblical way of understanding the world?

Homer the hedonist

Let's take a look at some of the main characters in *The Simpsons* to see how this might work. In the episode *Viva Ned Flanders*, Ned asks Homer to teach him the secret of his 'intoxicating lust for life'. Homer agrees, and is soon telling Ned that he has to stop thinking and start living 'in the impulse zone'. The pair find themselves in Las Vegas, where Homer leads the way in a succession of thrill-seeking adventures: Homer takes part in a daredevil show, recklessly sitting up at the wrong moment and risking the life of daredevil Lance Murdoch; he gambles all of Ned's money away; he gets Ned drunk and then discovers that both he and Ned have got married to cocktail waitresses. While Ned tries to find an honourable and decent way out of the last of these predicaments, Homer is running for the exit. When Homer and Ned are finally thrown out of town (they don't like people cheating on marriage vows in Las Vegas, apparently), Homer starts concocting an elaborate story of alien abduction to explain his and Ned's absence to their original wives.

Homer's instruction to Ned ('if you want to be like me, you've got to make snap decisions') is revealing, but it is the nature of those snap decisions that helps us to see what makes Homer tick. He lives for the pleasure of the moment – whether the pleasure is derived from danger, money or 'our good friend alcohol'. Homer's impulses show little regard for anyone other than himself. So Homer's worldview – on the evidence of this episode, at least[6] – is a selfish one of unbridled hedonism.

But Homer is just one character. *Viva Ned Flanders* can also be considered from the perspective of Ned: he has doubts about his morally upstanding ways, and his attempts to learn the ways of excess lead only to disaster.

There is no doubt that Ned would have been better off had he carried on as he was and never asked Homer for his help.

Critics of *The Simpsons* who point to Bart and Homer's reckless and irresponsible behaviour miss the point that although the main characters almost invariably get out of whatever trouble each episode throws at them, they also rarely end up ahead. Episodes that start with the family enjoying great good fortune finish with the status quo restored, just as the ones that start with disaster end in rescue or escape.

Nevertheless, by looking at the values that underpin each character's behaviour, we can begin to see which worldviews are on display and what conclusions the writers of the show suggest about them. All of this may seem like hard work, but it doesn't have to stop us enjoying the show. Homer's antics are just as funny when you understand the philosophical basis to them as when he's just a fat, bald guy who likes beer and doughnuts.

Christians in the cast list

And what are we to do with our new-found recognition of the values underpinning our favourite programmes? We need to see how they relate to the people around us. Although few of us are likely to know anyone quite as thoroughly impulse-led as Homer Simpson, we may well be able to think of friends of ours who live primarily for pleasure, or who are quick to think of themselves and slow to consider the needs of others. We may even recognise something of those attitudes (or others that we see on TV) in ourselves.

And the Bible tells us that we are to live lives that are distinctive from those around us. This means change –

notice that we are told to not conform any longer to the pattern of this world. The implication is that we used to conform to it. And most of us, even if we have been brought up in Christian households, are probably guilty of that to a greater or lesser extent. But what is the point of this change that we are told to make? Are we to mark our distinctiveness by rebuking our friends for not being as good and as distinct as we are? Are we to go out of our way to berate the lax morals of the world, as seen on TV? Probably not. Allow us to suggest an alternative response.

It is interesting that when Paul talks about the pattern of this world, the examples he gives in chapter 12 focus on our attitude towards ourselves, and to other people. We are told not to think too highly of ourselves (Romans 12:3); not to be too proud, but rather to be willing to spend time with people of low position (Romans 12:16). We are to show love, and to honour others above ourselves (Romans 12:10). We are to hate evil and cling to good (Romans 12:9) and to seek to live at peace with everybody, leaving all thoughts of revenge in the hands of God (Romans 12:19), who – unlike us – always judges rightly. All this gives us a clue as to what we are supposed to do with our distinctiveness.

The biblical pattern of thinking and living that is described in chapter 12 of Romans (and elsewhere throughout the Bible) is good for us, but is arguably not primarily for our benefit. The purpose of our distinctiveness is to glorify God, and to do so for the sake of those around us.

We could use our conclusions to start discussions with our friends: 'Did Chandler do the right thing? Why did he do that? Do the reasons for our actions matter anyway?' But we must also live in such a way that our friends will notice that we don't fall into the same mould as their favourite TV characters. The chances are that if your thinking is different to the model put forward by TV, it will also be different to the pattern that many of your friends fall into.

Many of our Christian friends have often complained at the absence of genuine Christian characters on long-running TV shows. *EastEnders* has tried to introduce various vicars over the years, as well as some lay characters who are identified as Christians. Most if not all of these have eventually revealed themselves to have feet of clay, or are portrayed as interfering do-gooders who try heavy-handedly to impose their morality on everybody else. Probably the most positive examples of Christianity on *EastEnders* come from Dot, who is also responsible for some of the worst and most unhelpful stereotyping. In other soaps, characters who develop an interest or awareness in religion are mocked by their peers (for example, Karen McDonald in *Coronation Street* and Bombhead in *Hollyoaks*,) with the implication that you have to be a bit strange to be at all religious. If only there was an authentic Christian character, we cry – they would stand out so clearly from the rest, and it would be such a fantastic advertisement for the gospel. But that thinking misses the point. Instead of complaining about the woolly-minded well-meaning stereotypes, or the blatantly unfair hatchet jobs that crop up on TV, perhaps we should be more concerned with a different type of soap opera, one where an authentic Christian role model is easy to add to the cast list and where it can have a significant impact: our own lives. If we are serious about living the kind of life that would make an impact if shown on *EastEnders* or *Coronation Street*, God can use us to make our friends think about the difference that following Jesus makes. But only if we are willing to stand out, to learn how to live according to a different pattern.

Study questions:

What are your favourite TV shows? What are the values that seem to underpin them?

Watch an episode of your favourite show and make a note of all the things that one particular character does. What is the meaning and significance of these events? What underlying worldview does this present?

What worldviews seem to characterise the programmes that you watch? To what extent do you recognise these worldviews in the attitudes of your friends?

How do you think your friends would answer these questions? Why not ask them?

Notes

1 President Bush was addressing the Republican National Congress. Actually the feud could be considered to have started two years earlier when the First Lady, Barbara Bush, commented to reporters that '*The Simpsons* is the dumbest thing I have ever seen'. Fortunately peace was restored after a letter signed by Marge was sent to Mrs Bush, prompting the First Lady to apologise for her 'loose tongue'.

2 See appendix 3 for a Damaris study guide on *Friends*.

3 Yorke, John; *EastEnders: Faith, morality and hope in the community*; a presentation at the diocese of St Albans Bishops' Day Conference, 4 September 2002. www.stalbans. anglican.org/yorkepres.htm

4 Ian had secretly had a vasectomy. After Laura's death, Ian discovered that the operation had gone wrong and that baby Bobby really was his son.

5 For a fuller explanation of positive deconstruction, see Nick Pollard's book *Evangelism Made Slightly Less Difficult* (Inter Varsity Press, 1997) chapters 3–5.

6 This episode by no means misrepresents Homer, although there are many other episodes where he shows other, nobler and more thoughtful aspects of his character.

6

Dancing With Barry White
What Does it Mean to Be Transformed By the Renewing of Your Mind?

> Therefore, I urge you brothers [and sisters], in view of God's mercy, to offer your bodies as living sacrifices, holy and pleasing to God – which is your spiritual worship. Do not conform any longer to the pattern of this world, but be transformed by the renewing of your mind. Then you will be able to test what God's will is – his good, pleasing and perfect will.
>
> **Romans 12:1–2**

In *Ally McBeal*, the character John Cage had faced a dilemma as a young man. Academically gifted, his life was inhibited by a lack of social confidence, most acutely when women were involved. Cage's response was to turn to a greater authority, soul music legend Barry White. The legacy of this was that whenever Cage needed to prepare himself for his work as a trial lawyer, or for a date, or for any occasion where self-confidence was crucial, a soundtrack of one of Mr White's best-loved songs played in his mind. First Cage's head, then his shoulders, then the rest of his body would begin to move in time to the deep soulful rhythms of *My First, My Last, My Everything*. Eventually Barry's spell was well and truly cast, and John Cage could be seen lost in the music and shimmying around the washroom, the office, or wherever it was that he happened to be at the time. The Barry White dance was developed over several episodes, and in time other cast members were drawn in. Before too long the spectacle of the entire ensemble of principle characters dancing in unison around the washroom became one of the joys of the delightfully surreal show.

The point is that in order to function effectively in his professional and personal life, John Cage recognised that he needed to think differently. He needed to somehow take on the confidence of someone like Barry White. If only we could understand our world from God's perspective, if only we could take on the mindset of God as we steer a course through our lives. Romans 12 suggests that such a transformation is not just something useful for us, but it's something absolutely essential if we are at all serious about our Christian faith.

What is a Christian worldview?

Taking on the mindset of God isn't as simple as imagining a soundtrack and dancing around in an entertainingly uninhibited manner. We talked in the previous chapter about identifying the values and worldviews that define the TV shows we watch. How do we take on a Christian worldview? How do we make sure that when we look at the world, we are looking at it from God's perspective?

A worldview, at its simplest, is a way of making sense of how things are. A Christian worldview is one which corresponds to Christian belief and doctrine about God and his relationship with the world – including his relationship with us. There was once a time in Britain when you could assume that everyone would at the very least be familiar with how the Christian faith answered the big questions of the world (even if not everyone actively sought to live their lives according to those answers). Now many people are not so much rejecting the Christian worldview, as being completely unaware of what it is. Before we can talk about establishing a Christian worldview as our own mindset, we need to go back to basics.

The Christian worldview

1. God the creator is in charge:

God made the world, and made it well. He knows how it works and he is uniquely qualified to say how it is supposed to run. When Job's patience finally cracks and he asks God why he is suffering, God's response isn't to explain his ways to Job; it is to remind him who he is dealing with:

> Where were you when I laid the earth's foundation?
> Tell me, if you understand.
> Who marked off its dimensions? Surely you know!
> Who stretched a measuring line across it?
> On what were its footings set, or who laid its cornerstone – while the morning stars sang together and all the angels shouted for joy? (Job 38:4–7)

God is in charge because there is nobody else who compares with him, no-one else who can do what he does. In *The Simpsons* episode *They Saved Lisa's Brain*, an emergency forces the local branch of MENSA (Lisa, Principal Skinner, Comic Book Guy, Doctor Hibbert and Professor Frink) to take over the government of the town. Even though they are the intellectual cream of the Springfield crop, they prove themselves to be completely unsuited to the task, producing ludicrous rules and regulations and bickering amongst themselves. God is in charge of the world because, frankly, nobody else is up to the job. We couldn't have begun to make it ourselves (not least because we would need God to make us first) and we can't begin to sustain it without him. Without God in our understanding of the world, we get a hopelessly distorted picture of the way things are.

2. Humans are designed to live God's way

Humans are designed to live God's way. We get the best out of our lives when we follow our maker's instructions. But because of our sinful human nature, we instinctively want to do things our way instead. To get the best out of our bodies we need to eat good food and take exercise, rather than just sit in front of the TV eating junk food. But for some of us, the sofa and the Pizza menu are too appealing, and we are far from our ideal weight. Whether or not you recognise yourself in the above description (you may shun fast food and have the body of a bronzed Adonis, much like the authors of this book), it is fair to say that the attitude we describe is true for all of us in some aspects of our lives. What is best for us isn't always what is most convenient for us, and we have a tendency to avoid the hard work required to change.

In the *Red Dwarf* episode *Bodyswap*, Rimmer (the dead hologram) persuades Lister (the lazy slob) to lend him his body. Rimmer's argument is that as Lister has no discipline or self-control, a two-week loan is his best option for getting back into peak condition. Lister agrees and, for a time, becomes a hologram while Rimmer occupies his body. Unfortunately, Rimmer was being less than honest about his intentions. Rather than hone Lister's flabby body, Rimmer is more interested in gratifying all the physical sensations that he has been deprived of since his death, and sets out on a gluttonous frenzy of eating, drinking and smoking fine cigars. When a horrified Lister reclaims his body, Rimmer is so hooked on the sensations of having a body again, that he drugs Lister as he sleeps and has the mind-swap procedure performed again.

When someone becomes a Christian, the Holy Spirit comes to live inside them. This doesn't mean that we have an arrangement like Rimmer and Lister's! Lister thought that by agreeing to give Rimmer a time-share on his body, he could cut corners in getting back in trim. The Holy Spirit doesn't do all the work for us, what he does is to stand alongside us, encouraging us to keep going and helping us to see where we need to change. He helps us to recognise what's going on when our fallen human nature leads us away from pleasing God, and he helps us to do the things that we know we should be doing. Unlike Rimmer, the Holy Spirit is true to his word. He does his work without forcing himself on us, deceiving us or getting distracted from the job in hand. And we need his help, because without it we wouldn't even be able to recognise our need to be transformed from our self-obsessed, sinful way of looking at the world.

3. *God reveals his way to people*

But with the help of the Holy Spirit, we can discover how God wants us to live, and discover the people he wants us to become. God reveals himself in any number of ways in the Bible – as a burning bush, through the words of his prophets, even on one occasion putting his words into the mouth of an ass. But there are two main ways in which we can expect God to communicate with us: through the words of the Bible, and through the example of Jesus.

– God's word revealed in the Bible

God is consistent, he doesn't change his mind on things. If something is wrong today, it's wrong tomorrow. He isn't like Reverend Lovejoy in *The Simpsons* who abandons his opposition to gambling, reasoning that once the government legalises something, God approves of it.

Because God is consistent and unchanging, we know that the principles behind the lessons in the Bible are reliable too. The practical application of how we love our neighbour may change as technology brings us into meaningful contact with more and more people in the global village, but the principle is the same – it's just that we are aware of a lot more neighbours. Developing a Christian worldview means recognising that if we want to please God, we should be reading his word to find out what he wants from us.

– God revealed in Jesus

In Colossians 1, Jesus is described as 'the image of the invisible God'(Colossians 1:15). Jesus himself told his disciples that 'anyone who has seen me has seen the Father' (John 14:9). If we want to know what God is like, what his values are, we need only look to the person of Jesus. When Jesus became a human he became (among other things[1]) a walking, talking, breathing example to us of how to live in a way that recognises that God is in charge.

And the most important example we should follow is Jesus' humility. In Philippians 2 (in a passage urging the church at Philippi to think of one another rather than insist on their own needs being met), we are told that although Jesus was 'in very nature God' he didn't grasp after equality with God. Rather he willingly set aside his place in heaven in order to be born as a human. As if this wasn't enough, he humbled himself to suffer physical death. And not just any physical death, but the most painful and shameful death imaginable – death on a cross. Why did Jesus do this? Because his nature was to make himself a servant: a servant to needy humanity and a servant to the supreme will of God the Father.

That example is an extremely challenging one for us to follow. If we take these words seriously, they will affect every part of our lives. If we are to humbly lay our lives down and submit to God's will, recognising him as our rightful ruler and Lord, then everything we do will need to reflect that Lordship, including our TV habits and including our thinking. We need to take on Jesus' mindset if we are to relate to God's world the way he intended.

Working hard at thinking straight

This chapter is all about our mindset, but we also need to remember that God wants us to make the most of the things he has given us, including our minds themselves. We have to work hard at developing the muscle we call the brain. Here are some practical suggestions for how we can do that.

1. Do it yourself

One aspect of modern life is that we are all consumers. Where once people had to make their own entertainment, now we can just settle back in front of the TV and have it all done for us. Where once people slaved away cooking a meal, now we can just slap a ready-meal in the microwave, and be fed in a few minutes with a minimum of effort. As Christians we can find ourselves adopting a similar approach to our spiritual lives. We allow the minister of our church to do all our thinking for us. We don't take time and effort to think through an issue, we just wait for the minister to preach on it and tell us all the answers. This is as misguided as the man who thinks he gets all the exercise he needs by watching *Match of the Day*. We need to rediscover the truth that we have to learn to think for ourselves. This isn't to say that we should ignore anybody else's input – far from it – but neither should we depend on somebody else to do all our thinking for us. When we read the Bible for ourselves, we should always be asking questions about how we apply what we read to our own lives. When we face a difficult situation at work, we should be asking ourselves what biblical principles we should bring to bear on our decision-making. We can't expect all the answers to be given to us by somebody else.

2. Don't do it all yourself

No, this doesn't contradict the previous point. We have already seen that Jesus promises that the Holy Spirit will help us to change and to grow. When we are working hard to think for ourselves, it's vital that we ask for the Spirit's help. We need to be open to the Spirit teaching us. All the intellectual development in the world is of little use if our minds aren't helping us to get more like Jesus. We want renewed minds based on God's truth, not just any old new minds. Philippians 1:9–11 suggests that our growth in insight is a gradual one: Paul prays that the Philippians will 'abound *more and more*' (our italics). As we work and God works in us, we can expect to see a gradual change in our thinking as we develop the mind of Christ (1 Corinthians 2:16).

We also need to enlist the help of other people. Wise Christians can help us to negotiate our way through difficult topics, and help to correct our thinking when it goes awry. Whether these people are the writers of Christian books or more mature friends of ours, we need guides for the paths of our study. Home groups or other small group Bible Studies can help us on the way as well. We also need to engage with people whose views on subjects will be a challenge to us. It is tempting to avoid talking to people who aren't Christians about issues until we are sure that we have got everything worked out. We don't want to be shown up and made to look stupid. Yet we shouldn't be afraid of the possibility that, on any particular issue, our non-Christian friends and work-colleagues may be right where we may be wrong. If our friends see that we are willing to recognise our errors, it will go a long way to convincing them that we are more interested in truth than in bludgeoning them into submission or bulldozing them into the kingdom of heaven. And the very act of honestly working through issues with someone who doesn't share all our presup-positions will help us enormously as we seek to develop the tools of a renewed mind.

3. Set targets

It is easy to be vague and unstructured in our growth. J P Moreland[2] has observed that it is impossible to decide to believe something – we either believe it or we don't, and no amount of coercion will make us accept something that we just don't believe to be true. However, Moreland continues, we can choose to undertake study of a particular issue in order to discover more and to see whether our initial position is misguided. For example, if we are not convinced that there is any truth in theories about evolution, we cannot simply decide that we will believe them anyway (at least, not with any intellectual integrity). What we can do is to read more widely on the subject. We can look at what scientists have to say, read appropriate parts of the Bible and relevant commentary material and then come to an informed opinion. It may be that our initial doubts turn out to be justified, or that they are put to rest and we find that we have changed our minds.[3] The important thing is to identify the things that we need to learn more about in order to discover truth, and then set ourselves to studying them. Quite apart from the issues we are thinking through, we will also be developing the skills that enable us to critically assess ideas that we encounter elsewhere – such as when we are watching television.

4. Think as you watch

And all of this, of course, has to come back to what we watch on television. As the previous chapter has shown, we need to bring our minds to bear on our favourite programmes, identifying the underlying worldviews that drive each show. What does each show get right and what do they get wrong? Are there any trends that can be seen across a wide range of programmes? How do these things relate to the gospel? How do they relate to the way we live our lives? Or to the way our friends live their lives? Part of being transformed by the renewing of our minds is developing a sense of 'joined up' thinking, a sense that every part of our lives matters to God, and every part plays a part in the process of our renewal.

This may seem like hard work, but we should keep two things in mind: first of all, that it is an ongoing process and we can't expect to ever be the finished article (at least, not this side of heaven). And God doesn't expect us to get it all right all the time. What he wants is for us to make the most of what he has given us, to develop our minds together with him and to devote them to his service. Which brings us on to the second point: contrary to much popular opinion, God does not want to tie up your mind with 'thou shalt nots'. He doesn't want to restrict you. He wants to liberate you. He wants to set you free from the distorted picture of reality that sin leaves us with. He wants you to think clearly, truthfully and to enjoy life in all its fullness – the life that he created you to enjoy – with him. And he wants to set you free to discover his will for your life, but more of that in the next chapter.

Study questions:

How would you explain the Christian worldview to one of your friends?

What helps you to critically assess what you see on TV? How can you develop your critical thinking about TV?

How aware are you of God transforming your mind? What are you going to do to try to develop a mind which is more godly?

Notes

1 Jesus is, of course, more than just an example to us. The little matter of his death and resurrection making it possible for us to be forgiven and put right with God shouldn't be overlooked. Nevertheless, his moral example is an important factor in how we are to understand Jesus.

2 Moreland, J P, *Love Your God with All Your Mind*; (Navpress Publishing Group, 1997).

3 If evolution happens to be an issue that you feel you need to do some more thinking about, one helpful book which doesn't push a single perspective is *Three Views on Creation and Evolution* (ed. J P Moreland and John Mark Reynolds. Zondervan Publishing House, 1999) in which Christians who subscribe to three differing viewpoints seek to demonstrate the strength of their respective cases.

7

Will and Grace
What Does it Mean to Test and Approve God's Will?

Therefore, I urge you brothers [and sisters], in view of God's mercy, to offer your bodies as living sacrifices, holy and pleasing to God – which is your spiritual worship. Do not conform any longer to the pattern of this world, but be transformed by the renewing of your mind. Then you will be able to test what God's will is – his good, pleasing and perfect will.

Romans 12:1–2

The TV series *Doctor Who* returned to our TV screens in the first half of 2005. Actor Christopher Ecclestone became the latest in a long line of actors charged with portraying the eccentric Time Lord, careering through time and space, fighting evil and opposing injustice. Throughout the long history of the show, the Doctor has frequently come into conflict with his own people, the Time Lords, who prefer to be observers (as opposed to participants) in the great conflicts of the galaxy. At one point, the Time Lords caught the Doctor, and his punishment for breaking their laws was exile on earth.

The problem wasn't that the Doctor didn't know what the Time Lords wanted. He knew perfectly well that they didn't want any of their kind getting their hands dirty in other people's business. The problem for the Doctor was that he didn't agree – he thought the Time Lords were wrong in failing to use their powers to help people in need.

There is a difference between knowing somebody else's will, and approving it or agreeing with it. The final phrase in our key passage from Romans 12 requires us to do both. We are to test God's will, and to approve it. As we work hard – with the Holy Spirit prompting, encouraging and challenging us – to become more like Jesus, verse 2 tells us that we will be able to test and approve God's good, pleasing and perfect will. But what does that actually mean?

Testing God's will

As we have seen, working out what God wants us to do in any particular situation isn't necessarily obvious. We will have to work hard to discover Biblical principles and apply them to a twenty-first century world, a world that is very different from the time when those words were first written. But we can at least be sure that God's values and God's principles hold true for all time. When we try to identify God's will, we can be sure that it won't suddenly change on us.

The TV show *Due South* centred on the relationship between Benton Fraser, an idealistic constable in the Canadian Mounted Police on secondment with the Chicago Police Department, and Ray Vecchio, his hard-nosed and cynical new partner. But suddenly, after two series of the show, a new actor started playing the part of

Ray. Rather than do what most shows do to cover up a change of this nature – just pretend that nothing has changed – the creators of *Due South* had some fun with the conventions of the medium. The old Ray (it eventually transpired) was on a new assignment, working deep undercover trying to infiltrate the mob. The new Ray was in fact another detective who had been assigned to take over Ray's identity, and he acted as if nothing had changed, as if he was the same old Ray Vecchio. Meanwhile Fraser was confused by the sudden change and, for a time at least, had no explanation for why his friend had suddenly been replaced with a counterfeit.

We can sometimes feel like Fraser, cut adrift in a world that quickly moves on and which leaves our old assumptions out-dated and redundant. But God isn't like Ray Vecchio. He doesn't suddenly change, and neither do his values. We can be sure that what God said yesterday about how we should live is what he will say today is what he will say tomorrow. God's principles are unchanging. That doesn't mean that we won't have to apply those principles differently as the world changes, but the principles themselves remain the same. We can be sure of God's unchanging character, and that provides us with a stable base for how we live our lives.

Although the Bible was written in a very different cultural setting to our own, we can still depend on it when working out how to live our lives. 2 Timothy 3:17 tells us that the Bible enables God's people to be 'equipped for every good work'. The Bible may not mention the Internet, tax-deductible work expenses, professional sport or even TV, but it does have something to say about all of those aspects of modern life. The God who rules the world has also revealed his will to us, and we should work hard at discerning how it applies to the minutiae of our lives.

Approving God's will

When we were small children, our parents may have told us not to sit too close to the TV set, or to not watch certain programmes. Some of us may even have done what we were told, but others of us will have ignored these instructions. The problem isn't in knowing what Mum and Dad wanted us to do, it was that we didn't approve of the instruction, so we wouldn't carry it out.

It can be the same with God's will for us. Once we discover God's will, we are faced with the choice of whether or not to obey. We can produce all sorts of reasons not to, but in the final analysis it comes down to this: if we say that God is in charge of our lives, if we recognise that he is a perfect, loving God who knows and wants what is best for us, then we have to act on the things we know that he wants us to do. Approving God's will means not only agreeing that his way is best for us (even if it isn't convenient); it also means putting it into practice in our lives.

So what is God's will for us?

Many of us tie ourselves up in knots trying to discover God's plan for our lives. Should I take this job or that one? Should I stay in my hometown or move to the big city? What happens if I make the wrong choice? What if God wants me in the city and I stay in my small town – maybe I'll never meet the person I'm supposed to marry if I stray from God's plan for me.

Philip D. Jensen and Tony Payne, in their excellent book *Guidance and the Voice of God*[1] describe God's will as being more like a compass than a map. We often think of God's plan for our lives as being intricately plotted, involving every major decision of our lives – where we should live, what job we should do, who we should marry, and so on – and live in fear of taking a wrong turn, being left with 'plan B' and a lifetime of missing out on God's best for us. It is true that God is interested in every aspect of our lives, but it isn't necessarily the case that everything is mapped out. God's compass shows us the direction that our lives need to be heading in – in everything we do we should be seeking to become more like Jesus. There are some decisions where there is a clear right and wrong option according to God's will – murder will always be wrong, as will adultery – but there are other matters where it really doesn't matter. To take one specific example, in choosing a career, we should consider the particular gifts that God has given us, but to some extent God is not worried whether we become a doctor or a farmer. But he is concerned that having decided to pursue either of those careers, we conduct ourselves in a godly way within our professional lives. We are to pursue righteousness, living God's way. God's plan for us has more to do with leading us into righteousness than it does with leading us to any particular preordained 'right' job, or house or even spouse.

Where we can be sure of God's will, is his will for everyone that he has chosen as his. There are four things that we can confidently say about God's will for all of his people:

- He wants us to experience his grace.
- He wants us to become more like Jesus and be presented before him, perfect in Christ on the last day.
- He wants us to become his disciples.
- He wants us to be active in helping others to do the same things.

He wants us to experience his grace

As our outline of the story so far in Chapter 1 showed, our situation without Jesus is a bleak one. The only hope we have of enjoying a restored relationship with God is if he acts to make things right, it is completely outside of our power to make amends. Fortunately, by sending Jesus to die for our sakes, God has done just that. God's will for his people is to experience his extraordinary grace in coming to die for our sake, so that we could be forgiven. We are to put our faith in Jesus' death as the full and final payment for everything we have ever done against God.

He wants us to become more like Jesus and be presented before him, perfect in Christ on the last day

But God doesn't lose interest in us when we put our faith in Jesus. We may think of becoming a Christian as the end of a long process, but in fact it is just the start of a new adventure.

The West Wing usually finishes each series with something of a cliffhanger. The first series finished with a shooting, and in the confusion of the scene, viewers had to wait for the first episode of series two to discover which of the regular characters had been shot. The second series ended with President Bartlett, his administration thrown into chaos by the announcement to the world that he was suffering from multiple sclerosis, about to announce whether or not he would run for a second term. The third series finished with Bartlett finally taking the decision to have a foreign cabinet minister/terrorist assassinated, the fourth with him temporarily abdicating his position due to the kidnap of his daughter Zoë, and the fifth with tensions in the Middle East on a knife edge and another member of Bartlet's team fighting for their life. In each case, as well as bringing the series to a tense and gripping conclusion, the cliffhanger also turns the action in a new direction that leaves the viewer eagerly anticipating the new series. Becoming a Christian works in a similar way. The moment of our decision to put our faith in Jesus feels like an end-of-series climax, but it also turns our lives in a new direction, and should give us a sense of anticipation for what comes next. Becoming a Christian is more about the beginning of the new series than it is about the end of the previous one.

Colossians 1:28 talks about Christians being presented before God on the final day, perfect in Christ. God views us as perfect now, because of Jesus' perfection, but he also wants us to grow and to take on more of Jesus' godly character. While it is true that we aren't going to reach perfection this side of eternity, God doesn't want us to sit around idly while we wait. We are to start now, letting God reshape us and restore in us his image, the image that we have spoiled with our selfishness and sin.

At this point, we should add that God knows our weaknesses and he knows when we fail. The chances are that most, if not all, of us have watched things that we wish we hadn't, and have chosen to watch things that we know we shouldn't. God doesn't ignore or dismiss our sin, but he does forgive it. If we are willing to repent, to say sorry to God and to make a fresh attempt to live his way in our TV watching, we can be sure that we will receive his forgiveness. Don't give yourself a hard time over your past failures in the area of TV, but don't give in to repeating old mistakes either.

He wants us to become his disciples

God isn't interested in just winning converts, pulling in the cosmic equivalent of record viewing figures. He wants disciples, people who are committed to living their lives for him rather than for themselves. As we have seen, this means bringing every part of our lives under his control, and it's hard work. Colossians 1:29 brings together the dual nature of this struggle:

> To this end I labour, struggling with all his energy, which so powerfully works in me.

We have to work hard in order to be Jesus' disciples, but as we do so, God gives us the strength we need to carry out his work. It is our struggle, but we don't have to depend just on our own strength.

He wants us to be active in helping others to do the same things.

And we shouldn't be so selfish as to think that we are the only ones who God is interested in. The last recorded words of Jesus in Matthew's gospel have him telling his disciples to 'go and make disciples of all nations'. The primary task of someone who is serious about being a disciple is to make more disciples – to help others to hear about God's grace and to help them to grow more like Jesus themselves.

That is God's will for his people: to know his grace, to become more like him, to be disciples and to make disciples. That is what we need to test and approve.

God's will for our TV viewing

So how does what we watch on TV help us – and others – to get more like Jesus?

How does watching TV help us to know God's grace?

Even when we have been Christians for many years, it is easy to take God's grace for granted, forgetting just what an amazing thing it is that he has done for us. Or we can slip into thinking that we will be all right when we finally stand before our judge, because of all the good things that we have done for him. We need to remember not only how much God has given for our sake, and what he has saved us from, but also of how helpless we are to do anything about our situation ourselves. We need to orientate our minds around the fact that we have received God's amazing grace, and live in the light of that.

Much of the programming that we see on television today depicts a world that doesn't recognise God's grace, and we can either become conditioned to think in the same way, or we can use those programmes to remind us of what our lives might be like without Jesus. We should never stop thanking God for what he has rescued us from, but neither should we be content to leave it at that.

How does watching TV help us to become more like Jesus?

Hopefully reading this book has helped to answer that question already. It is our view that TV shouldn't be dismissed as a mere distraction from more fruitful activities for Christians. As we watch TV we should be taking part in a two-way conversation. We need to hold our beliefs up to what television displays of the world's attitudes. We also need to test and refine our understanding of our faith in the light of the things that we watch. Not that this means bending our belief to fit the philosophy of our favourite shows, far from it. But rather, we should be applying our belief to the ideas and values of our culture, as revealed on TV and elsewhere, and in the process growing in our understanding of what it means to follow Jesus. Clearly, we can't expect TV to do the whole job for us, and if we never switch the TV off and spend time with the Bible and with other Christians, we shouldn't be surprised if we end up being more like the characters of our favourite soap opera rather than more like Jesus. But as we become more aware of God's standards and his will for our lives, and as we learn to think critically about what we are watching, we will find that even TV becomes another tool that our creator can use to shape us according to his will.

How does watching TV help us to become better disciples?

As with any other part of our discipleship, we have to work hard at our TV watching. We have to grapple with questions about whether watching a particular show is compatible with living out our covenant relationship with God. Sometimes it will be obvious that particular shows are unhelpful to us and inappropriate viewing for a disciple of Jesus. But there will be lots of other TV shows that are not so clear cut. The one sure statement is that if we don't think about what we are watching, if we don't consciously include God in our viewing, then our TV watching will have little benefit to us or to God's kingdom. As with every part of our lives, we should be seeking to glorify God in our TV viewing. If we are serious about accepting God's rule in our lives, that means the whole of our lives.

How does watching TV help us to help others to become disciples?

But the Christian life is not one that we live for our own benefit. And this is one of the strongest arguments for Christians not cutting themselves off completely from the world of television. Whether we like it or not, TV provides many of the talking points in modern life. When work colleagues gather together at lunchtime, or on a coffee-break, or just as they pass in the corridors, a significant number of the conversations will begin with 'did you see. . .' If we haven't seen the shows that everyone is talking about, it makes it so much harder to be part of those conversations. And if we aren't taking part in those conversations, how can we find opportunities to point people to Jesus? When missionaries are preparing to go out to foreign countries, they spend an enormous amount of time learning about the culture they are going to be living in. There is a recognition that if they want to communicate the gospel clearly, they have to be able to relate it to the cultural environment that the people they meet are familiar with. We live in a world more media-saturated than at any time in our past, and if we are serious about reaching people with God's unchanging gospel of grace, we need to be able to talk their language – the language of TV.

We need to work hard at making sure that TV is a tool

for our own development in godliness and not something that will corrupt and stunt our spiritual growth. We also need to work hard at understanding the issues and worldviews that underpin our favourite (and our not-so-favourite) shows. If we can develop the ability to translate what the shows are really saying, to recognise the values and messages that the shows are insinuating, then we can help our friends to think about those things and question whether or not they really agree with them. TV can provide a fantastic opportunity for Christians to talk about the difference that Jesus makes in their lives, or what he has done for us.

The authors of this book like TV, but we love Jesus. We don't think that those two statements need to be incompatible. But if we are serious about getting more like Jesus, we have to make sure that we keep our priorities the right way round. By all means, reach for the remote control and enjoy some television, but don't leave your mind on standby while you are watching, and don't forget what you've watched as you go out into the world for God.

Study questions:

How does your TV watching help you understand more of God's grace?

What is your understanding of God's will for your life? How does that relate to what you watch on TV?

What have you learnt about watching TV from this book? What have you learned about sharing your faith with other people?

Do you think that TV can help you to become more like Jesus? What else do you need?

Notes

1 Jensen, Philip D and Payne, Tony, *Guidance and the Voice of God* (Mathias Media 1997). See pages 96–98.

Appendix 1

Culturewatch Groups
By Caroline Puntis

My own memories of joining a Culturewatch Group[1] are significant enough to stand tall in my mind some seven years later. One dark evening in a church in Southampton, a group of Christians gathered together in contemplative study of a very popular book. But it wasn't the Bible. In fact, this was no Bible study group, prayer group or planning meeting. We were there to discuss John Gray's *Men Are from Mars, Women Are from Venus*[2] (thankfully no longer on every coffee table). I remember thinking the kind of thoughts that could have ended my connection with the Damaris community there and then – What on earth are these people talking about? How can I possibly say anything useful? Why didn't I make more of an effort to finish reading the book?

I suspect I'm not the first or last person to have had this experience. My first meeting felt like I was stepping out of some of my favourite comfort zones into the relative unknown. I could talk about TV, films, books and music until the cows came home, and I was used to discussing issues from a Christian perspective – I just hadn't ever put the two together before. Thanks to an excellent leader, however, I managed to battle through my self-doubt and emerge a confident, shining example of – wait a minute, that's not how it happened.

Thanks to an excellent leader, however, I eventually got a word in edgeways. I believe I made a ridiculous statement along the lines of, 'Well, I think it would be better if men were more like women,' and to my surprise the discussion continued. I realised that I was in a safe place where I could speak and people would listen without judgement. I felt unhampered by what I thought I should say, or what I would say if I were someone else (the kind of person who knows what everyone is talking about, always has something useful to say and who finished reading the book).

I also found that after a while I began to 'tune in' to the Damaris style of analysis. We weren't just talking about the book as a piece of literature, we were talking about the ideas presented in themselves. We even went one step further and talked about how they related to what we felt the Bible had to say on these issues. Perhaps this approach is more clear cut when you consider a conversation about a film – far from being limited to remarks such as, 'I thought Brad Pitt couldn't act to save his life,' a Damaris discussion is more likely to question how his character made certain choices and why.

And this is where I got hung up initially – thinking that you have to be a serious intellectual to process a harmless piece of entertainment in such a way. As you have hopefully discovered for yourself in reading this book, there is no such thing as harmless entertainment. Everything has a controlling idea that deserves some attention. Some things warrant an in-depth exploration of the underlying messages – which is where Culturewatch groups come in.

We want to thoughtfully consider the impact of

influential programmes on TV, such as *Friends*, in a way that will help us to connect with the real world where we spend most of our time. But it is not our intention to simply make moral statements about TV shows – the kind that would be of little help when talking to a friend who doesn't share our beliefs. We want to engage, rather than judge. To this end, the real aim of the groups is to become a bit more like Jesus in the way we handle the worldly ideas that are constantly jostling for attention in our brains. We want to work out how to behave so that people notice the difference Christ makes in our lives. And we want to be able to talk about our faith in a way that doesn't make a nation of TV-lovers yawn and nod off.

So if you're seriously into making a difference and want to do this in a fun way, why not think about joining – or even starting – a Culturewatch Group? Hopefully the answers to these 'frequently asked questions' will help you on your way.

Frequently asked questions

Why does Damaris organise Culturewatch groups?

By now, if you haven't come across Damaris[3] and its resources before – or even if you have – you may well be wondering what the name Damaris has got to do with people meeting up to discuss contemporary culture.

Damaris was a lesser-known Greek lady who gets a mention in Acts 17: 'A few men became followers of Paul and believed. Among them was Dionysius, a member of the Areopagus, also a woman named Damaris, and a number of others' (verse 34, NIV).

How did Damaris become a Christian? In a nutshell,

Paul was in Athens waiting for Silas and Timothy to join him. He took the opportunity to join in the daily discussions about anything and everything at the market place. He had something particular on his agenda, however, and began to tell them the good news about Jesus. Word got back to the Areopagus[4] that a new teaching had emerged and Paul was hauled in to account for what he had been saying. Rather than blasting them with a forty-minute sermon on the authenticity of Jesus, Paul eased his way in with a look at their own culture of idols. Using his knowledge of their beliefs, he presented the gospel in a way that was relevant – even including a line from one of their own poets (Acts 17:28). Paul's teaching about the one true God was delivered in a way that made sense to Damaris and others who found faith that day.

The Damaris Trust produces resources that relate our culture and Christian faith. We hope that they will help many people to explore what it means to follow Jesus Christ. Culturewatch Groups are a practical way for Christians everywhere to engage in the issues that preoccupy the world today, and to discover new ways of communicating their faith. If you're not a Christian, they're a good way to find out how relevant the Bible is to contemporary issues.

The Culturewatch[5] website is one of the resources produced by Damaris to help individuals and groups as they consider the issues being raised in contemporary culture. There are many study guides which are written primarily to be a resource for Culturewatch Groups to use, and you will find four TV-related examples at the end of this book which should give you an idea of what to expect. Groups also find that Culturewatch articles give them valuable help in identifying what to look at. And of course, group members have many ideas of their own.

Who goes to Culturewatch Groups?

The short answer to this question is, 'anyone'. You just need to have a grain of interest in contemporary culture (books, films, TV, music) and talking about your faith with people who aren't part of a Christian community. The groups are fairly small – between five and twelve people is the ideal size. They could be people with a common area of interest; they may be from the same church or perhaps from several churches. Alternatively, you might not be a Christian but would like to hear some more about Christian faith from an angle you're familiar with.

Where do they meet?

Most groups tend to meet in people's houses – just like a Bible study or home group. For convenience, groups may choose to meet at church, or even the local pub! There's nothing to stop you meeting anywhere that lends itself to relaxed conversation.

Are all the groups the same?

No. There is no set pattern and nobody is going to check up on you to make sure you're doing everything 'right'. Some groups may find that they have a particular focus – perhaps they only look at films, or books (pop music is not everybody's cup of tea!). It could be, however, that the diversity of a group is the focus and people come along to learn from others' expertise.

Who decides what the group is going to study?

Usually, the leader will have a few suggestions up his or her sleeve if the group cannot come up with something they would like to study. Hopefully, they can then decide together.

Do I need to have done lots of preparation in advance?

Not necessarily. Obviously, if you have managed to read the book, see the film, watch the TV programme or listen to the album, you will get more out of the discussion. But there is nothing to stop you turning up on the night without a clue. You can still listen and contribute if the issues raised are something you feel you can talk about.

How often do the groups meet?

Every few weeks, but it really depends on the group and possibly the material. It could be that a group chooses to meet up again in a month's time, if they are going to study a film next, but a thick non-fiction book may require a longer gap.

How long are the meetings?

Typically a couple of hours, depending on the size of the group and how much people have got to say.

What happens at a Culturewatch Group?

At the groups I have attended things don't usually get going until a round of drinks has been served, along with some informal chat. The leader would then start the meeting with a prayer and possibly a Bible passage that relates in some way to the issues raised by the chosen material. For the benefit of those who haven't managed to come fully prepared, someone will summarise the book, film, TV programme, etc. The leader will then chair an informal discussion. The meeting usually closes with a short time of prayer.

What sort of questions will be asked in the discussion?

Once you have explored your own impressions of the material (a good way into meaningful discussion is often through initial comments such as, 'I thought it was rubbish!'), things should be taken onto the next level.

Damaris suggests five ways to approach either individual study or group discussion:

1. Identify the underlying worldview: What beliefs, values and attitudes are being communicated?
2. Analyse the worldview: Do these ideas make sense? Do they fit with the real world? Do they work?
3. Affirm truth: What rings true with Christian faith as seen in the Bible?
4. Identify error: What seems to be inconsistent with Christian faith?
5. Identify a response: How should we respond to this material or this worldview as individuals, as a church, as a community?

The first four elements make up the process known as 'positive deconstruction'. You can read about this in *Evangelism Made Slightly Less Difficult* by Nick Pollard.[6]

How do I find out if there's a group near me?

Culturewatch Groups generally seem to have a natural life of about three to four years, so the number of groups is constantly changing. I would visit the Damaris discussion forum to see if someone has posted a message about a group in your area. If there is one, then you should make contact directly via the discussion forum or by email to the contact person.

If there are no groups near me, how do I start one?

There are several stages to starting a group:

1. Confirm that your personal Christian faith and practice is consistent with the Damaris Statement of Beliefs – we require all group leaders to do this, since they are representing Damaris. However, of course, we do not require the group members to agree with this.
2. Sign up for Culturewatch Update – a free weekly e-mail newsletter informing you of new study guides and articles on the Culturewatch website.
3. Find some members! You could recruit ten or so members yourself, or you could find three people who are really enthusiastic about the idea and get them to each recruit three more. You could post a message on the Damaris discussion forum to see if there's anyone else in your area who's already interested.
4. The most effective way of launching new groups is to run a Damaris Workshop[7] as a launch event. You could book one for your church or open it up to others. Please contact the Damaris office[8] if you need more help.
5. Download the brief guide to leading Culturewatch Groups from the Damaris website.[9]

Notes

1 Or a Damaris Study Group, as they were called then.
2 *Men Are from Mars, Women Are from Venus* – a practical guide

for improving communication and getting what you want in your relationships (Thorsons, 1993).

3 Go to www.damaris.org for all the latest resources relating contemporary culture and Christian faith. Click on the 'church' menu to find information relating to study groups.

4 The Areopagus considered themselves to be chiefly responsible for the introduction of any new religions or foreign gods.

5 Go to www.culturewatch.org, or you can access the site through www.damaris.org.

6 Pollard, Nick, *Evangelism Made Slightly Less Difficult* (IVP 1997).

7 A member of the Damaris team can be booked to come and speak to your group about Damaris and study groups. More information is available at www.damaris.org/damaris/pg_church_workshops.html.

8 Send an email to office@damaris.org for more information.

9 All of this information on study groups, and more, is available through www.damaris.org/damaris/pg_church_studygroups.html.

Appendix 2

Study Guide on *The Office*
By Ian Hamlin

Written and directed by: Ricky Gervais and Stephen Merchant.
Starring: Ricky Gervais, Mackenzie Crook, Martin Freeman, Lucy Davis, Ralph Ineson, Patrick Baladi, Ewan Macintosh.
Broadcaster: BBC
First series: 2001
Key Concepts: Work and workplace relationships, boredom, self-awareness, popularity, ambition, success.

Summary

The Office, an acclaimed comedy series without stars, a laughter track or much plot, is tightly focused on the inhabitants of one work place. The office in question is that of Wernham Hogg, a Slough-based paper supplier – but it could be anywhere.

The action, such as it is, is based around the employees. Dawn: dreamy receptionist, engaged to warehouseman Lee yet frequent flirter – especially with Tim, a sales rep who is more aware than the rest of the mind-numbing tedium of his job. Then there's Gareth, team-leader, seeker of girlfriends and proud standard bearer for the Territorial Army who has an air of ridiculous self-importance made bearable only by his extreme naivety.

For the second series, these stalwarts were joined by a larger group, recently re-located from Swindon – an amalgamation which provides the source of such story there is. These recruits include Neil, the dynamic and effective new boss; Rachel, a new love interest for Tim; Brenda, a disabled woman; and Oliver, a black man, with the presence of the latter two characters resulting in issues of political correctness being thrown into the pot.

All of these people are managed by the show's central character, David Brent (Ricky Gervais). As office manager, Brent exudes enthusiasm and incompetence in equal measure. Full of management jargon and a desire to 'entertain' as well as manage, his excruciating attempts at team-building consistently end in disaster. Each episode takes us on a cringing journey of embarrassment by means of office gossip, half-formed romances, failed attempts to impress, thwarted ambitions and sheer repetitive ordinariness. We share in his humiliation as he loses his job and seeks to re-emerge on the D-list celebrity circuit. Finally, in the two Christmas specials (first shown in 2003) we sit, teary-eyed, at an unanticipated, subtle, yet gloriously fulfilling happy ending.

Background

'The greatest programme ever seen,' is how Richard Curtis, creator of *Blackadder*, described *The Office*. High praise indeed for an odd little comedy series set on a Slough industrial estate produced by two previously unheard of writers (Ricky Gervais and Stephen Merchant) who brazenly insisted that they not only write up their idea but direct it as well. Yet *The Office* has become a soaring success, from an almost immediate cult hit with an initial following of 1.5 million for its first summer showing on BBC2, to BAFTA and international award winning critical acclaim, record breaking DVD sales and a 5 million audience for the start of the second series. The final triumph was Gervais' lifting of two Golden Globes – an unheard of triumph for a British show on American TV.

This success certainly reflects the fact that *The Office* is funny, but there seems to be more to it than that. Most reviewers have spoken of how the hilarity is, at times, almost unbearably painful to watch. 'A middle-management *Twelfth Night* . . . confronting us with fallible, half-witted existence . . . capturing to perfection the boredom, sniping and pettiness that are so much a part of life . . . a fierce distillation of every lousy trait . . . complacent mediocrity in anxious decline . . . a comedy of ordinariness.' Put like that it doesn't sound much fun. Yet the humour comes from an easy identification, a ready recognition of just how painfully real this all is.

The Office, then, is truly a comedy of our times. It reflects the importance of work in the lives of so many, the hopes that are invested in it as well as the disappointment as it invariably fails to deliver. It examines human relationships in all their messy and comic minutia – the 'romance' between Tim and Dawn has been examined, through both series, with hardly a word of meaningful dialogue, everything expressed in a furtive glance or a raised eyebrow. It harshly exposes the shallowness and pretension of so much everyday behaviour, glibly covered up with jargon, political correctness or petty one-upmanship. It echoes all of our desires to be popular – not only respected but liked – loved even.

If Christian faith is to be real and relevant today, it needs to be seen in the myriad of places just like Wernham Hogg, and work for the people who spend their lives there.

Study questions

1. What parts of *The Office* do you recognise from your own workplace experience?

2. Most reviewers describe *The Office* as both hilarious and painful to watch. Do you think this is true? Can it be both? How does the one side affect the other?

3. Ricky Gervais has said that he wanted to write something 'that felt like real life'. The comedy deals with 'daily sameness' and 'life as a condition we plod through day after day'. Do you think this bleakness is truly captured? Are things really that bad?

4. Which of the following ongoing themes within *The Office* are the most poignant or ring most true in your experience? What is the series saying about them?

   a) petty rivalry and gossiping

   b) office romance/jealousy

   c) management jargon

   d) political correctness

5. David Brent is the latest in a line of British comedy characters, including Captain Mainwaring (*Dad's Army*), Basil Fawlty (*Fawlty Towers*) and Victor Meldrew (*One Foot in the Grave*), who epitomise a sort of sad pomposity. What are Brent's defining characteristics? Is he good or bad, happy or sad? What does he most want in life?

6. What is it about Neil that makes him appear to be a better boss and a more rounded person?

7. It's been said that *The Office* embodies the spirit of our time, not least because it is set, not in a family or among friends as with traditional sitcoms, but in the workplace where most Britons spend most of their lives. Is work a place where people hope to have their wider, emotional, spiritual needs met? Can it ever provide these things? Can work colleagues provide the sort of support and acceptance which may, in the past, have come from other places?

8. Tim, in some ways, represents the ordinary person in this office. He sees it for what it is and wants more, yet is unable to break free from the security it offers. How easy is it for dreams and ambitions to get lost in the regular and the mundane?

9. In the concluding Christmas episodes, did the ending surprise you in what was largely a bleak picture of office life? Did it ring true, and do you think those brief glimpses of happiness are what many people strive for as means of hope, even redemption, from the drudgery of the routine or the failure of bigger dreams?

10. What do you think David Brent's favourite Biblical book or story would be? What passages does his character bring to your mind?

11. How ought a Christian approach his or her workplace? What might they say or do in an office like this one to make a difference?

12. How can the church better equip people for their daily working lives?

Appendix 3

Study Guide on *Friends*
By Caroline Puntis

Created by: Marta Kauffman and David Crane.
Starring: Jennifer Aniston, Courteney Cox Arquette, Lisa Kudrow, Matt LeBlanc, Matthew Perry, David Schwimmer.
Producer: Warner Brothers Television
Broadcaster: Channel 4 (UK), NBC (USA)
First Series: 1995 (UK), 1994 (USA)
Key Concepts: Relationships, independence, ambition, success, failure, growing up, comedy, happiness.

Summary

Friends is the ongoing comic drama of the lives of three guys and three girls living in New York City. Since their debut on the small screen, Ross (David Schwimmer), Rachel (Jennifer Aniston), Joey (Matt LeBlanc), Phoebe (Lisa Kudrow), Monica (Courteney Cox Arquette) and Chandler (Matthew Perry) have all made the transition from twenty- to thirty-somethings. On an individual level, progress in other areas has not been so consistent. Ross has achieved some success in his career and is currently lecturing at NYU in Palaeontology. Personally, however, he is a disaster. At the end of series 9, he has three ex-wives and two children by different women. The love of his life, Rachel, is the mother of his second child – they live together, but are not having a 'relationship'. Chandler, on the other hand, has finally found success in his marriage to Ross's sister Monica, but has yet to find a job that suits him.

The characters who seem to have changed the least are perhaps Joey and Phoebe. Joey is a struggling actor who, apart from falling in love with Rachel during series 8, has no qualms about remaining single – his main passions in life are eating and having sex. In series 9, Phoebe finally realises that she has never had a long-term relationship and decides it is time to change. She is perhaps the most independent of the group, having worked her way off the streets onto the middle-class stage occupied by the others.

The motto of the series is probably best summed up in the *Friends* theme tune, 'I'll be there for you . . .' Through thick and thin, this group of disparate individuals turn to one another for support – although they are united in putting their own interests first. The random tragedies that beset the friends are always played out to comic effect, leaving the impression that the pain of real life will never catch up with them.

Background

Finally ending after ten seasons, *Friends* was undoubtedly a huge success story. Much of the credit must go to the actors who have helped to develop the characters over the years. The show was originally conceived by Executive Producers Marta Kauffman and David Crane after they graduated from university and moved to New York.

Ted Cohen, one of the show's many Executive Producers, sums up the change that the characters have to go through: 'Nobody wanted to have these characters stay in their 20s forever, that wouldn't be true. The challenge is to do things that are organic for characters of this age, and have it remain entertaining.' In other words, how does the show move from being about carefree twenty-somethings to mature adults with responsibilities – and remain funny? It seems that the show's writers have achieved this in part by moving some of the characters on, whilst holding others back – Rachel and Ross have a baby, Monica and Chandler get married; Joey continues to have relationships with no commitment.

The producers were determined that the presence of baby Emma should not kill the atmosphere. 'The baby's gonna sleep a lot,' said Shana Goldberg Meehan. 'That's the challenge, is to have a baby on the show and have it feel like *Friends*.'

Celebrity culture is part and parcel of the *Friends* world. Episodes have featured guest appearances by big stars such as George Clooney, Jean-Claude Van Damme, Chris Isaak and Julia Roberts. Jennifer Anniston in particular has become a huge celebrity, partly due to her marriage to Hollywood star Brad Pitt – he appears in one episode as an old school friend of Ross who always hated Rachel (series 8, *The One With The Rumor*).

Quotes from www.signonsandiego.com/tvradio/long-runningnbcprograms.html

Study Questions

1. How do the writers get people to tune in to *Friends* week after week, year after year . . .?

2. Discuss each of the characters: what are their main strengths and weaknesses?

3. To what extent do the friends depend on one another for their happiness?

4. What pressures do the friends face in their daily lives?

5. How are the characters shaped by their family backgrounds?

6. What have the six friends got in common? How are they different?

7. What are the major changes the friends have gone through since the first series (e.g., in terms of lifestyle, attitudes and relationships)?

8. To what extent was the final episode a satisfying conclusion for long-term fans of the show?

9. Are the characters stereotypes? If so, how?

10. In what ways is the group a community?

11. How does the city provide for the friends?

12. What are the tensions present within the group?

13. What does the show say about boy-girl relationships?

14. What are the truthful elements of *Friends*? What is untrue?

15. Does *Friends* deal with serious issues? How?

16. What effect does the comedy have on the characters and their situations? How do comedy and values interrelate?

17. How are friendships different to family ties? What would you say to someone who believes that they only need friendships with people of their own age and interests?

18. Identify the key needs of 'Generation X' (people now in their twenties and thirties). How are they motivated? What does the Christian community have to offer them?

19. Compare the community of *Friends* with your church community.

20. How would you share the Gospel with someone who is genuinely very happy and successful?

21. The show's producers admit that the characters could never afford the rents on their apartments. What lifestyle values does *Friends* validate? How do you think the show influences its younger audience? What are the implications?

Appendix 4

Study Guide on *The West Wing*
By Steve Couch

Created and written by: Aaron Sorkin.
Starring: Martin Sheen, John Spencer, Stockard Channing, Bradley Whitford, Allison Janney, Richard Schiff, Janel Moloney, Dule Hill, Rob Lowe (seasons 1–4), Josh Malina (from season 4), Gary Cole (from season 5), Jimmy Smits (from season 6).
Broadcaster: Channel 4 (UK), NBC (USA).
First Series: 2000 (UK), 1999 (USA).
Key themes: Politics, integrity, compromise, honesty, relationships, power.

Summary

The West Wing focuses on the professional and personal lives of the closest advisers to the most powerful man in the world, the President of the United States. Josiah Bartlet is an intelligent, charismatic, quick-witted Nobel prize-winning economist who has surrounded himself with a team of idealistic staffers eager to be a force for good in America and the world. Although each show immerses you in the minutiae of the American political system, you don't have to be a constitutional expert to follow the plot. At the heart of the show are the characters – President Bartlet and his team of advisors. As Martin Sheen (who plays Bartlet) says, 'If the audience doesn't care about these people they won't get the series. One must be drawn in by them, to their work, to their individual personalities, to their individual characters, to the struggles in their personal lives. They come from a place and they stand for something.' (Foreword to *The Official Companion to The West Wing* (Warner Bros 2002).)

Background

Aaron Sorkin had previously written the screenplays for major film releases *A Few Good Men* (1992), *Malice* (1993) and *The American President* (1995). The latter film, about the romantic relationship between the President of the United States and a political lobbyist, was in many ways the starting point for what became *The West Wing*. Sorkin's original draft of the movie screenplay was three times as long as it needed to be, and he still wanted to tell the stories of the senior staffers that never made it into the movie. When John Wells approached Sorkin about writing a television show, he knew what he wanted to write about.

Originally the President himself was going to be a recurring background character – someone who would be seen on screen maybe one episode in four, but Martin Sheen's brief performance in the pilot episode was so striking that it made Sorkin realise that the show needed the dramatic weight that including the President as one of the regular central characters would give it. Nevertheless, the show has always been an ensemble piece, rather than a vehicle for one or two star performers. The first season holds the record for the most Emmies won by a series in a single season, and the show has won the Outstanding Drama Series Emmy for four consecutive years, as well as a host of other television awards.

Characterised by Sorkin's sharp, intelligent, witty scripts and by the powerful and emotive end-of-season cliff-hanger episodes, *The West Wing* has built up a loyal following despite the erratic scheduling that it has suffered in the UK (season 5 began airing on Channel 4's digital channel E4 in July 2004, despite the terrestrial mother-channel not airing season 4 until November 2004). Season 4 also marks the point at which other writers began to produce some of the scripts, as Sorkin was struggling to keep up with the hectic production schedule of the show.

Study questions

1. Which of the main characters do you most closely identify with?

2. Which episodes of the show particularly stick in your memory as favourites? Why?

3. 'I don't have a political agenda with this show. I don't write this show so I can step up and mouth off about what's bugging me this week. It is based on what's writeable, really. I'm most comfortable writing when there are two people in a room who disagree with each other. It can be about the time of day, but they have to disagree and each of them has to have a point' (Aaron Sorkin, *The Official Companion to The West Wing*, p.125). Do you think that *The West Wing*

manages to give both sides a fair hearing, or is it skewed to the Democrat/ liberal agenda pursued by Bartlet's administration?

4. '*The West Wing* isn't meant to be good for you . . . Our responsibility is to captivate you for however long we've asked for your attention' (Aaron Sorkin, www.pbs.org/newshour/media/west_wing/sorkin .html). Does TV have any duty beyond entertainment? What responsibilities do the makers of television programmes have to their viewers? And to their society? What responsibilities do we have as viewers?

5. Current affairs issues tackled in various episodes include: African AIDS relief; the environmental responsibilities of large corporations; sexual and racial discrimination; responses to terrorism; American foreign policy doctrine; the death penalty; and the importance of filling in census forms. Do shows like *The West Wing* help you to think about big issues, or is the political backdrop purely a matter of entertainment?

6. 'It is more important than my marriage. Right now, these few years, while I'm doing this, yes, of course it's more important than my marriage.' (Leo McGarry, *Five Votes Down*, season 1). What are the most important things in your life? Do you agree with Leo that being Chief of Staff to the President of the United States is more important even than his marriage? What other job (if any) is more important than someone's marriage?

7. At the close of season 4, Bartlett invokes the 25th

Amendment and temporarily steps down as President, because the kidnapping of his daughter Zoë has rendered him incapable of exercising his duties. How does this compare with Leo's sacrifice of his marriage in season 1? Which of the two men made the correct judgement, or were they both right? What are the differences between the situations?

8. Several characters have difficult relationships with their fathers – CJ Cregg's father has Alzheimer's disease; Toby Ziegler struggles to forgive his father for his activities as a gangster in the 1950s (*Holy Night*, season 4), and before the birth of his twins Toby voices fears that he might be unable to love his kids the way other fathers do (*Twenty Five*, season 4); President Bartlett is haunted by his relationship with his dead father, who was cold and hostile towards his intellectually superior son. What makes relationships between parents and children difficult? How do relationships between fathers and their children impact on our relationships with our heavenly Father?

9. Several episodes turn on moments of personal loyalty between the main characters. What factors earn such loyalty in real life? How important is loyalty? Who or what do you feel that you are loyal to?

10. The flashback scenes in the episodes *In the Shadow of Two Gunmen parts 1 and 2* (season 2) show how each member of the President's staff came to be part of his campaign team. What seem to be the main factors that drew them to work for Bartlet? Are there any parallels with the decisions of Jesus' first followers to

go with him? (See Mark 1:14–20; Mark 2:13–17; Luke 5:1–11 and 27–32.)

11. America's Christian Right is criticised by characters in several episodes; a Republican offers to save the President's Foreign Aid Bill, in return for a tiny amount of funding for a medical study into the efficacy of prayer (*Guns Not Butter*, season 4); Bartlet's Catholic faith recurs as an integral aspect of his character and Presidency; after the death of Mrs. Landingham, Bartlet rails against God as 'vindictive' and a 'feckless thug' (*Two Cathedrals*, season 2). What picture does the show paint of Christian faith?

12. In several episodes the view is expressed that, at least in part, the Bible is outdated, with certain parts of it needing to be ignored or dramatically reinterpreted for modern life. How would you respond to an argument along these lines?

13. Leo McGarry: 'This is the most horrifying part of your liberalism – you think there are moral absolutes.' President Bartlet: 'There are moral absolutes' (*We Killed Yamamoto*, season 3). Who is right? What are the implications of either point of view to everyday life for ordinary people (as opposed to Presidents and their advisors)?

14. 'The issue of the show, to an extent, every week – and here's where the metaphors get mixed – is, how dirty do your feet have to get without suffocating yourself in the mud in order to get an inch of what you really want done?' (Bradley Whitford, www.pbs.org/news hour/media/west_wing/whitford.html) To what extent are you willing to compromise on certain

things in order to 'get an inch of what you really want done'? Which areas of your life (if any) would you never compromise on? What are the implications of compromising or of not compromising?

15. 'I think it's what they hope life is like in *The West Wing* because these are all good people trying to do the right thing' (Allison Janney, www.pbs.org/news hour/media/west_wing/janney.html). Is Bartlet's White House your idea of an ideal administration? Which aspects of it would you like to see mirrored in real life? Which aspects would you not want to see?

16. Should President Bartlet have got away with the non-disclosure of his Multiple Sclerosis?

17. 'You can't play a President. The other players have to treat you like one. That's the only way that you have any credibility. So I'm very lucky that they treat me with a degree of respect. At least on camera' (Martin Sheen, *The Official Companion to The West Wing*, p.195). To what extent is authority dependent on the reaction of others? To what extent does this apply in the same way to all of the following: political leaders; religious leaders; God?

Appendix 5

Study Guide on
Desperate Housewives
By Louise Crook

Created and written by: Marc Cherry.
Starring: Teri Hatcher, Felicity Huffman, Marcia Cross,
Eva Longoria, Nicolette Sheridan.
Broadcaster: Channel 4 (UK), ABC (USA).
First Series: 2005 (UK), 2004 (USA).
Key themes: Desperation, loneliness, love, relationships,
appearance and reality, happiness, money, friendship,
divorce, marriage, infidelity.

Summary

Desperate Housewives takes a darkly comic look at
suburbia, where secrets abound and life isn't quite what
it seems. Wisteria Lane appears to be a wealthy American
suburb like any other, with perfectly manicured lawns,
the smell of home baking and smiling residents who are
completely content with their suburban lives. This façade
is a myth, however, which is shattered a few minutes into
the first episode. Everyone assumes that Mary Alice

Young (Brenda Strong) lives a happy and fulfilled life, until one day after 'quietly polishing the routine of my life until it gleamed with perfection' she takes out a revolver and commits suicide. From beyond the grave she offers us an enlightened narration on the lives of her friends, and is to be our guide for the rest of the series.

Susan Mayer (Teri Hatcher) is a divorcée whose husband left her for his secretary. She is desperately searching for love, and when Mike Delfino (James Denton), a handsome widower, moves to Wisteria Lane she decides to try to attract his attention. However, despite the best efforts of her teenage daughter Julie (Andrea Bowen), things don't seem to go smoothly. Susan has to fight off Edie (Nicolette Sheridan), a predatory divorcée who seems determined to devour every eligible bachelor in the neighbourhood. More than that, Mike is not all he seems, and his secretive life proves another obstacle that Susan has to overcome.

When Lynette Scavo (Felicity Huffman) became pregnant, her husband Tom (Doug Savant) suggested that she give up her high-powered career to look after her children full-time because it would be 'much less stressful'. She soon discovered that being a full-time mum is not an easy option, and looking after four exuberant children under the age of six means that her life is so hectic she hardly has time to think. Before too long she is addicted to her boys' Attention Deficit Disorder medicine and at the end of her tether. Even when she resorts to poaching a nanny from another family, she soon finds that life is as difficult as ever before.

Bree Van De Camp (Marcia Cross) is a domestic goddess. Everyone in Wisteria Lane regards her as the perfect wife and mother, except for her own family. Her husband Rex (Steven Culp) is fed up with 'living in a detergent commercial' where everything is perfect and where Bree acts like she is 'always running for the mayor of Stepford'. When Rex asks for a divorce, Bree obsesses about what the neighbours might think and refuses to address their marital problems. Family life further unravels as Bree and Rex enter an uneasy alliance to keep son Andrew's involvement in a hit-and-run accident a secret.

Finally, Gabrielle (Eva Longoria) is married to Carlos (Ricardo Chavira), a successful and massively rich businessman. A former model, Gabrielle was promised by Carlos when they got engaged that he would provide her 'with everything she wanted'. The only problem is, as she herself says, she wanted all the wrong things. In her loneliness, she seduces her seventeen-year-old gardener John (Jesse Metcalfe) and flirts with disaster in her attempts to keep their affair a secret. Even worse, when Carlos is arrested Gabrielle realises that she will have to work for a living.

The writer of the show, Marc Cherry, has described *Desperate Housewives* as the story of 'four women in the suburbs going slowly mad'. Each of the four women faces a different set of trials, and experiences a different flavour of desperation as their stories intertwine with one another and the steadily increasing degree of mystery and conspiracy surrounding events in Wisteria Lane.

Background

Desperate Housewives has been dubbed the new *Sex and the City* and has taken both America and the UK by storm. The first episode shown in the US pulled in 22 million viewers, and the show has helped turn around the struggling ABC network on which it is shown. In the UK, the first episode drew 5 million viewers, beating the rating figures for the premiere of both *Friends* and *Sex and the City*. It won the Best Television Series (Musical or Comedy) Golden Globe Award 2005, and Teri Hatcher (who plays Susan Mayer) won the Best Performance by an Actress in a Television Series Golden Globe.

Desperate Housewives has been described by actress Nicolette Sheridan as '*Sex and the City* meets *Twin Peaks* meets *American Beauty*.' Because it pokes fun at typical American family values, it has not been well received by some on the American right. Several big advertisers pulled out of the show after pressure from family values pressure groups. However, writer Mark Cherry has said of the show, 'I'm not judging this world. I embrace the world, I love it,' and has found it hard to see what the fuss is about. Despite this controversy, the current ratings on both sides of the Atlantic suggest that *Desperate Housewives* is here for the foreseeable future.

Study questions

1. What do you think of *Desperate Housewives*? Why do you think it has been so popular both in the UK and the US?

2. How would you describe the show to a friend who hasn't seen it? What do you think the underlying themes of the show are?

3. What do you think of the opening sequence? Why are Adam, Eve and the forbidden fruit from the Garden of Eden used in this sequence?

4. Which character do you most identify with and why?

5. What do each of the four main characters have in common, and how are their struggles similar? How are the characters and the struggles they face different? Do you think that the emotions shown by the main characters reflect the real life experience of most women?

6. To what extent do you think *Desperate Housewives* poses a threat to family values?

7. What perspective of marriage does *Desperate Housewives* present?

8. What does *Desperate Housewives* have to say about being a full-time mother? Does it affirm or undermine this role? How do you think our society values the role of full-time motherhood?

9. How is religion portrayed in the show? Consider such events as Bree reading the Bible (and then putting it away) when faced with Andrew's hit-and-run, and Mrs Huber's response when confronted by Paul Young over her blackmail note to Mary Alice.

10. What is the effect of having the show narrated by the deceased Mary Alice?

11. Why is Bree so obsessed with appearances and being the perfect housewife? Has she achieved the perfection she longs for? What has her search for perfection cost her?

12. How does Lynette feel about her job as a full-time mother? How does she compare this to her previous job as a high-flying career woman?

13. Why do Susan and Edie engage in a childish fight to win Mike's attention? Why is it so important to Susan that she gets a date with Mike?

14. Why is Susan initially unable to forgive Carl for what he has done to her? What effect does this lack of forgiveness have on Susan, Carl and Julie? What helps her to finally forgive and move on? How important do you think our society thinks forgiveness is?

15. Why did Gabrielle marry Carlos, and what impact has this decision had on her life? Is she happy?

16. What do you make of Carlos and the way he treats Gabrielle? What drives him? How do you feel about him?

17. Why is Gabrielle having an affair with John? What do you think about the affair and the morality of it? How do you think our society regards infidelity?

18. What was your reaction when Susan confronted Gabrielle about her affair? Would you ever do something similar if someone you knew was committing adultery? Why?

19. Why does Bree decide to break the law by covering up Andrew's involvement in the hit-and-run incident? Why does she subsequently phone the school to tell them about Andrew's stash of marijuana? What connects these seemingly contradictory decisions?

20. Mary Alice tells us in episode three that she lived in

fear, but that 'to live in fear is not to live at all'. She believes that her friends are all living in fear. What are they each afraid of? How would the biblical teaching that God is in control of everything and longs for us to enter into a personal relationship with him impact this fear?

21. What do you think the desperate housewives are searching for? How would an understanding of Jesus' invitation 'Come to me, all you who are weary and burdened, and I will give you rest' (Matthew 11:28) help these characters? How will you let this teaching help you in your struggles?

About the authors

Nick Pollard is co-founder of the Damaris Trust. Having trained as an academic psychologist and started various businesses, he worked with the Billy Graham Association for a while before founding his own ministry. He is the author of *Teenagers: Why Do They Do That?*, *If Only: The Search for Happiness* and *Evangelism Made Slightly Less Difficult*, as well as contributing to a number of other books for a variety of publishers. Nick is married to Carol, and they live in Southampton with their two teenaged children, Luke and Lizzie. Nick's favourite TV shows are *Fawlty Towers* and *Time Commanders*.

Steve Couch was a church youth worker for nine years before joining the Damaris Trust as Managing Editor of www.relessonsonline.com. He is also Managing Editor of Damaris Books and the series editor of the popular *Thinking Fan's Guides*. He lives in Bournemouth with his wife Ann and their young son Peter. Steve's favourite TV shows are *The West Wing* and *Match of the Day*, but Peter prefers *Ballamory*.

Teenagers
Why Do They Do That?
by Nick Pollard

Concerned about teen drug-taking, pregnancies and eating disorders? Baffled about what drives many teenagers to such behaviour? Worried that 'it must be my fault'?

This brilliantly enlightening book argues that understanding the culture in which teenagers are growing up is the key to understanding why some inflict tragedy upon themselves or others.

Nick Pollard, a specialist in teenage spiritual and moral education, provides adults with invaluable insights to enable them to open doors of communication with teenagers and begin to influence them for good.

If Only:
The Search for Happiness
by Nick Pollard

'If only I were rich and successful. If only I were free to do whatever I wanted, whenever I wanted. If only I were healthy and secure. Then I would be happy. Then I would be content.'

We spend our lives searching for fulfilment – but are we looking in the right places?

This book tells the true-life stories of three people in search of an answer. Andy wants to be a millionaire and doesn't care how many people he treads on – until he is faced with his own mortality. Sharon wants to be free to use her body and the bodies of others – until she ends up in a brothel. Jacqui thinks she will be happy when she forms her own stable, secure family – until personal tradgedy strikes.

In reflecting on their experiences, Nick Pollard comes to some surprising conclusions.

Matrix Revelations
A Thinking Fan's Guide to the Matrix Trilogy
Editor Steve Couch

The first in the *Thinking Fan's Guide* series, providing in-depth analysis of the ideas behind the Matrix films written for fans of the films by fans of the films.

Groundbreaking, innovative and much imitated, the Matrix trilogy represents the most talked about cinematic experience in recent years. Unrivalled in uniting serious philosophical thought with serious box office, *The Matrix*, *The Matrix Reloaded* and *The Matrix Revolutions* occupy a unique place in popular culture.

Matrix Revelations examines the *Matrix* phenomenon, with in-depth analysis ranging from the science fiction and comic book influences to the philosophical and religious themes that underpin the films.

www.damaris.org/matrix

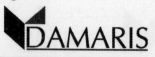

Coming Soon

DAMARIS

"Relating Christian faith and contemporary culture"

Back In Time

A Thinking Fan's Guide to Doctor Who

by Peter S. Williams, Tony Watkins and Steve Couch

(due for publication autumn 2005)

DAMARIS